NEVER

NEVER

Jens Pulver

And the Wednesday Group
that Will Change
the World

Timothy J. McKinnon

iUniverse, Inc.
New York Lincoln Shanghai

Never
Jens Pulver
And the Wednesday Group that Will Change the World

iUniverse books may be ordered through booksellers or by contacting:

iUniverse
2021 Pine Lake Road, Suite 100
Lincoln, NE 68512
www.iuniverse.com
1-800-Authors (1-800-288-4677)

ISBN: 978-0-595-43484-8 (pbk)
ISBN: 978-0-595-88300-4 (cloth)
ISBN: 978-0-595-87811-6 (ebk)

Printed in the United States of America

For all of the people who have entered my life
and shown me love.

~ Jens Pulver

To my wife, Michelle.
You remain the greatest gift I have ever received.

~ Timothy J. McKinnon

In my heart I found God.
Through God I found strength.
Through strength I conquered all.

~ Jens Pulver

Contents

Introduction

Jens Pulver, a world champion athlete, grew up in an environment few could imagine or comprehend. At a young age, he was forced to endure challenges and experiences that would cripple most spirits. Yet, even through intolerable verbal and physical abuse, Jens thrived because he had the incomparable love of his mother and a steadfastness about him that would carry him beyond life's greatest obstacles. Early on, he learned there would be no free lunches or easy roads. If he were to succeed, he would have to do so through hard work, effort, and suffering.

From a brutal beginning to an epic rise, Jens would be gifted with amazing mentors and trustworthy coaches. Monte Cox and Pat Miletich would sculpt this masterpiece, understanding that sweat could replace entitlements and pity must not exist. Jens became the UFC's (Ultimate Fighting Championship's) first lightweight world champion in Mixed Martial Arts (MMA).

There is nothing pretend about Jens Pulver.

He is unvarnished, authentic, individualistic, raw, inspiring, maverick, emotional, nonconforming, unpredictable, a walking contradiction at times, and yet, above all, he is real.

Never

At the age of thirty-two, he has seen and experienced more than most will throughout a lifetime, having overcome unimaginable odds and continuing to inspire everyone who is fortunate enough to learn *his story*. Whatever the world throws at him, whatever the future has in store for him, you can be sure he is equipped for the battle.

Little did Jens know, when he stumbled upon a few brothers in the back room of a sweaty gym, that his life would take on new direction. Burdens would lift, friendships galvanize, and his spirit be reborn. Thoughtfully, methodically, and deliberately, he and his brothers would set out to change the world.

If you have ever heard that achieving your dreams is unattainable, strap in for this ride. Jens Pulver's journey proves that anything is possible and no goal is too great. If you don't believe me, just ask Jens.

Preface

It would be a pivotal day in my life.

I wanted to run. The temperature in Bettendorf, Iowa, had been in the upper eighties and the heat index even higher. I had never been one who enjoyed the mundane. I've always preferred outside temperatures either ten below zero or ninety-five degrees. Ordinary just doesn't suit me; the more extreme the experience, the better. I had chosen black shorts, sunglasses, a ball cap, and my Livestrong wristband. After I grabbed my shoes and hurriedly splashed on sunscreen, I flew out the door. Within a minute or two, my heart rate bumped up against anaerobic levels. My route and the length of the endeavor were unknown. I just knew I wanted to run hard.

I was battling an idea that had spun in my head for weeks. No matter how determined I had been to shake it, it wouldn't let go. I had tried many times before to bury the idea into the hidden regions of my mind. On this day, however, it seized me.

Sixty minutes into the journey, I felt fatigue in my legs, which typically wouldn't exist at that juncture. The lactic acid had built up in my muscles, and my pace had been at the upper limits of my abilities. Yet, I kept up the pace mile after mile. I ran so hard that sweat poured from my body. Floods of sweat cascaded down my forehead and spilled into my eyes, stinging badly and blurring my vision. However, I didn't stop to wipe my face. I was afraid that, if I slowed, I might change my decision. I knew that, as soon as I returned home, I needed to sit down with my wife for one of those "we need to talk" talks.

I didn't know exactly how I would convince her that I needed to leave my career of nearly fourteen years and pursue a mission that existed in my heart. This would require a significant amount of faith. I would need to inform her that I was required to write a book. Required in the sense that I believed I was called to write it. I had to tell the world about Jens Pulver.

During my years as a business executive, I was fortunate enough to be in the presence of some of the finest, most highly respected teachers in the country. From professors at the J. L. Kellogg Graduate School, at Northwestern University, to Harvard University PhDs, with a few stops in between, I had encountered greatness. These men and women possessed credentials and academic pedigrees that warranted being on the boards of Fortune 500 companies. Yet, none of them had taught me more about life, resiliency, perseverance, success, failure, achievement, and endurance than Jens.

This is not simply a story about Jens Pulver. It is more. It is about his presence and influence in my life and the lives of many others. Whether you know him personally or only through the upcoming pages, you will never be the same. This is a tale of inspiration and a group of men with a desire to change the world.

This story is about all of us who drive for excellence, desire to be more, refuse to give up, yearn to be inspired, give of ourselves, strive for bravery, are determined to take power over our lives—everyone who has overcome adversity, everyone who wants to be relevant and necessary.

Never

As a child, how many times were you hit so hard in the face that you saw pure black?

Before your vision cleared, you were struck again, again, and again. Unrelenting, seemingly unceasing, closed-fist punches that continued to hit their mark.

You try to cover up, you scramble, you try to block the fury of blows; but somehow almost every one lands. Your jawline, eyes, and head receive these wicked intentions. You feel your face swell, taste your own blood, and pray that you will die. At least then, the pain would be over.

As a child, how many times did you see your mother brutalized? Savage beatings, more sinister than you could imagine.

She screams, moans, and pleads, to no avail. The rage is palpable. The chorus rings in your head. You know if you try to assist, it will be worse for both of you. You grab your head, pray to God that it stops. Then silence. It's hard to know which is worse: silence or violence. The only problem with dead calm is that you know how the movie ends. It might be temporarily over for now, yet it's simply the starting point of the next cycle. The calm before the next imminent storm.

As a child, how many times did you see your siblings psychologically or physically assaulted?

Perhaps worse than receiving a beating yourself, you are forced to listen to and watch as your two little brothers endure the same torture. Although you can barely defend yourself, your brothers have no chance at all. Their situation is categorically more insidious; younger and smaller, these boys understand even less. They have no idea why any of this happens. You remain helpless. You exist hopelessly. You wonder why. You question everything.

Now, imagine for a second the perpetrator is not a stranger. He is someone you know, the man who created you, the one who provided half of your DNA. The one who was supposed to protect, nurture, guide, care for, teach, and love you. Your father. Administering the entire gamut of almost unending cruelty is your father.

Even a child knows this shouldn't be so. How many times in your life can you relate to this type of pure evil? I hope never.

If you believed his father, Jens would never be …

significant
wanted
a good son
a good father
needed
substantial
relevant
noteworthy

He would never go to college, succeed, thrive, or be loved.

Never.

Unless you truly knew Jens, you would never know his ...

courage
fears
fierceness
fragility
spirit
demons
resiliency
pain
gentleness
loyalty

You would never see his kindness, intelligence, or heart.

Never.

Brackish

As an adult in the world of Mixed Martial Arts, he became known as Little Evil or Lil' Evil. This nickname has always caused me to pause. Until recently, I haven't been able to quite put my finger on why, perhaps because I have felt that Jens is not nearly Machiavellian enough to possess the moniker. If any part of Jens Pulver is evil, it's his left hook. You can prepare for most things in your life but certainly not that left hand. You can train, box, spar, whatever; but the first time it lands, you understand why so many have fallen before. The weapon can't properly be qualified as an art or a science—simply a unique experience of plain old blunt trauma, delivered especially for you. So, I concede, that left hand is a lil' evil.

Before Little Evil, there was Little Jens.

Have you ever tasted the barrel of a shotgun?

It can best be described as brackish: an unpleasant, yet memorable taste. Memorable in the sense that Jens believed the experience might be his last in this world.

At the seasoned age of five and a half, Jens found himself fighting back the caustic tang of gunmetal. His father had lined up Jens and his two brothers, in the living room, to once and for all conclude the final chapter of the Pulver family. It was time for Jens to leave this earth. Drunk out of his mind, his father would murder his family and swallow enough rat poison to end his own life. He would destroy his family and simultaneously leave a legacy of malfunction and failures. This was the easy way out, the only route he knew to travel.

It was an ugly day. Jens had a strange sense of ambivalence that flowed through him but wasn't particularly thrilled with the thought of dying. At the same time, the current daily curriculum was as bad as you might imagine. As he sat in his own urine and listened to the heartbreaking cries of his brothers, he felt as though time stood still. He tried to anticipate his father's nefarious motives and how long it would be until he pulled the trigger. Who would be first? Would he at least be quick and efficient between killings? Perhaps worst of all, if he didn't exterminate everyone today, what possibly could be next? The flood of uncertainty was enough to disable his senses.

Jens's mother recounted the horror that day: "I was sure he was going to kill all of us. His eyes were as black as the pits of hell. He wasn't just going to shoot my kids in front of me; he wanted to make the torture even worse. He kept screaming at me, 'You choose; you choose who I shoot first.' I had Jens on one side of me, Dustin on the other, and I was holding Able in my arms; he was just a toddler.

"He [the father] was frothing at the mouth, snot dripping from his nose, pacing back and forth with pure hate in his eyes. Jens had the shotgun on him most of the time, probably because he was the oldest. I closed my eyes and waited for the sound of the shotgun."

His father waged a forty-five-minute battle in his own head before pulling the barrel from Jens's face and staggering out the back door. Despite all the pain the man inflicted on the family, there was a queer sadness that came over Jens and his mother. On so many previous occasions, they had wished him dead. And now, their emotions just flatlined; it seemed so sad. If he was going to off himself today, what a waste, they thought. What a complete, utter, and pathetic waste.

As it turned out, he chose not to have an entrée of arsenic for lunch and sat outside and pouted. Outraged by his family's lack of attention, the father stayed in the backyard in a much-deserved pile of solitude. When he finally managed to wobble back inside, he slammed the door, hurled a few more insults, grabbed a bottle of liquor, and disappeared.

It is almost impossible to understand what leads a person to abuse his children. Jens said his father used to be passionate about riding horses. At the height of his career, he was considered a champion rider and as talented as any jockey in the Northwest. Yet what accompanied a lifetime of riding was a lifetime of cutting weight. To ride at this level, you need to be stealthlike, and lighter means better. When you naturally walk around at 140 pounds and are required to be 120, the pressure of losing significant weight is debilitating. Losing this daily battle can slowly destroy your life. The tactics necessary to shed these pounds on an ongoing basis are never healthful.

Since food and calories become the enemy, drugs are often the first and wrongheaded answer that floats to the surface. And although alcohol contains a gratuitous amount of empty calories, people somehow are fooled into believing that drinking is better than eating. Hence, you are left with a wicked combination of drugs, alcohol, and inevitable anger. These forces unite to form an imminent recipe for certain disaster.

His father was only twenty years old when Jens entered the world. Within seven years, Jens had three siblings. At the unprepared age of twenty-eight, his father had four children; he was addicted to drugs and alcohol and dealing with the pressure of a failing career. A few of his remaining characteristics included frequent rage, persistent anger, and a dead-cold bitterness. Looking back, Jens revealed, "My mom truly fell in love with my dad and had the hopes and dreams of raising a healthy family. He simply turned into a miserable SOB and managed to wreck everything we could have become.

"Since I was a little kid, I knew I would become a fighter. The strikes never hurt me. Each time I tasted a punch, it got my attention; but the pain was over quickly. It never lingered. The sh-t that always hurt the most were the blows to my heart. I'll destroy the biggest guy in the room, behave like an animal, bring your house down, rage against the machine, whatever; but do something that hurts my heart, and I'm done for."

Speaking softer, with a slow, disgusted shaking of his head, Jens admits, "I'm a crier; yeah, Jens Pulver, the crier. It's never the physical. It's when you attack my emotions, my feelings, and my being; that's the stuff that never goes away."

You're going to need more than a shotgun to keep Jens down.

Marlene

If asked who shared the most significant relationship in his entire life, Jens would answer, without pause, his mother, Marlene. Although she is a small lady with a tiny frame, her influence is immeasurably important. Through all of the abuse, suffering, and torment, she was always there for him. As his father's terror reigned, she wasn't always capable of physically defending Jens; yet her heart would restore his heart every time. No matter how dreadful life was at home, she managed to rescue Jens where it truly mattered, in the depths of his soul. Even though her husband had evolved into a cold, merciless, and bitter man, Marlene was the exact opposite. Grace, kindness, and love poured out of every ounce of her being.

When your brain has been corrupted with aggression and hostility, it's no longer about being physically tough. It's about surviving minute by minute, hour by hour, in a battle with your past. The thoughts, memories, and sheer ugliness of your prior existence clash in your mind and compete for space. Marlene was capable of replenishing this cerebral real estate with virtue and strength. Within seconds of hearing her voice, Jens's self-doubt would transform into perseverance. Her ability to renovate the family's daily challenges is even more remarkable when you remember she endured the same hideous attacks herself.

Many times, victims of abuse will succumb to the dreadful-ness and take one of two roads: they will continue the cycle of neglect and exploitation, or they will crawl into a corner some-where and give up. Neither option was acceptable for Marlene. She, like her oldest son, was not a quitter. She was a fighter. By whatever means necessary, whatever sacrifice required, she would survive, and she would thrive. It was part of her genetic makeup. Cruelty that would pound most giants into submission was not enough to shrivel this lady, not even close. Her plan was bigger. Her goals were necessary. Her kids were everything. The survival of her kids was everything.

In retrospect, Jens looked back and couldn't comprehend the sacrifices she made for him and his siblings. Jens explained, "She worked all the time. She worked so damn hard, she almost died. There were days where we would never see her; she would just drop by to leave groceries. Unbelievably, she kept us in a four-bedroom house on a few acres of wilderness. We hardly had any money. We had plenty of love, just no money."

Jens went on to say that some of his worst childhood memories were not about him. These were memories of his mother pleading for help or crying out at night after another beating. Just like her children, Marlene was also a victim and received some of the worst abuse imaginable. Because her husband was indiscriminate in terms of times and places, many were even delivered in broad daylight.

The family was at the race track, and, as was custom, booze and anger were also in attendance. Jens can't remember the exact, unprovoked reason, but his dad had decided to deliver another pounding. Scarcely able to say the words, Jens describes: "Dad was on top of her, beating her badly, and she was trapped under her chair. She couldn't defend herself or escape; she just took the blows, one after the other. Just as sick as what I witnessed was that no one got out of their chair to help. There were plenty of adults, watching the whole damn thing, and they all just stayed seated."

Jens pauses before finishing. "I don't understand that. I was a kid and they were adults; how could it be that no one helped her? How could that be?

"This is the same guy who would punch me in the face when he thought I did something wrong. He would kick me off my bicycle, if he felt I didn't ride it properly."

The father's logic was unsolvable, his motives a mystery. Jens wishfully states "All I ever wanted was to have a good relationship with him. I just wanted that d-ckhead to take me fishing one time. Is that too much to ask? Me and dad fishing, just one f---ing time."

As a young teenager, instead of owning memories of fly fishing in a tranquil stream, he had other visions. The Pulver family road trip was quite different from the gleeful story-books. He remembered a particular Thanksgiving Day when, by the conclusion, he was simply thankful to be alive. The family was rolling down the highway, and his brother Dustin was running his mouth. Jens explained: "It always seemed to be Dustin, stirring things up and making something go from bad to worse."

As his mom was driving, his father's rage meter had topped out, and it was time to leave the copilot chair and wreak some havoc, time for the boys to pay. After informing Marlene that, if she touched the brake pedal, the outcome would be worse, he started in on Dustin. Jens was asleep at the time and awoke to the terror that had just begun. Disoriented, groggy, and attempting to grasp the frenzied situation, the first thing he remembers hearing was Dustin getting slammed into the back door of the van. Almost by instinct, and just like so many times before, Jens got up to defend him. As he looked at his father, he recalls him saying, "Stay out of this or I'll kill you." Jens followed orders and was rewarded by getting punched square in the face.

Jens knew this confrontation would be different. All of those years of being on the receiving end of his father's rage would suddenly change. This time, he would fight back. He wasn't just going to sit back and endure another beating. He knew he would be entering the line of fire. He knew this wasn't a battle he started. He knew it was going to hurt. His personal well-being, however, was not the issue; that was secondary. He wasn't going to let his dad beat up his brother again, not today.

The father was nursing a broken nose that he received horse riding, so Jens planned to take advantage of this vulnerability. This illustrates the depths of despair, when a son is forced to contemplate the most effective means of injuring his father. However, it was either going to be Jens or him.

Jens recounted: *"Bam, bam, bam,* the punches started flying; it was such tight quarters, and he was standing over me, launching blows as fierce as he could. Anything I could use, arms, elbows, fists, knees, whatever I could think of, I threw. Despite the mayhem and chaos, despite noise and screaming, I managed to land a left cross square on his nose, with precision and exactness.

"Immediately, blood started spraying everywhere. I was able to open up a few more cuts and fought with everything I had. Now, it was about survival. I thought, damn, he's tough, that son of a bitch is so damn tough." As the van screamed down the highway, only the occupants inside knew of the pure hell that was taking place. To the outside world, as in so many other instances, no one knew the narrative. No one knew the truth.

By now, Marlene disobeyed the previous instructions to keep driving and pulled over to some dodgy, rundown rest stop. She felt desperate; if she didn't attempt to help, Jens might not survive.

His dad had determined that the misery, fury, and storm were not quite over. There was more anguish to administer, more cruelty to demonstrate, and more brain-searing memories to make indelible. Jens literally fell out of the van, and the abuse continued in the parking lot. This time, however, Jens didn't retaliate; he just covered up. His dad fired what seemed to be a hundred or more blows. Jens did nothing more than shield his head with his hands. Looking back, not even his most fierce and severe battle to become world champion was a brawl this intense, dreadful, or hideous. This was simply about life and death. He didn't know if losing this war also meant losing his life.

After more than ten minutes of beating on his eldest son, the father was now frustrated and tired. He was also disappointed that, no matter what he threw at Jens, he couldn't get him to break. Whether his dad had reached pure exhaustion or his blood-alcohol ratio caught up with him was unknown, but he staggered back to the van and collapsed. Marlene quickly gathered her traumatized children and assembled them back into the van. They raced off, in search of the closest restroom. It was time to clean up the mess. The blood from this battle could be wiped away, but the scars of the event would last a lifetime.

After finding the nearest gas station, Jens limped into the bathroom to wash his face. Marlene, sobbing at his side, helped drag Jens inside the door, his eyes caked with the scarlet red blood of his father—thick, pasty, and dried. Jens could barely walk, could barely see a thing. He was weary, fatigued, worn out, and his body broken to the core. He faintly had the will to remove the blood from his face. Today's war was over, but at what cost?

Jens, almost unable to verbalize the story, said, "What hurts me the most was not the punches I took that day. That sh-t never lasted. It was what my mom must have been thinking as she cleaned off my face. Can you imagine? There was so much blood. It was in my eyes, nose, and hair and had completely soaked my clothes. By now, it had seeped into the person that I would become."

His mom proceeded to remove the stains off her eldest son, ever so tenderly and with the gentleness and love of God himself. As if she were talking to her newborn, she began choking on her tears. Almost indecipherably, she whimpered, with a hushed voice, into his ear, feeling so much pain, so much guilt, and so much helplessness. He remembers her words spinning in his head: "I'm sorry, son, I'm sorry; I'm sorry, Jens, I'm so sorry, baby, Jens, I'm sorry, I'm sorry. I'm so sorry, baby, I'm so sorry."

Jens and his mother, Marlene

Self-Pity

This chapter is short, as there is no self-pity in Jens's life.

Motley Crew

I met Jens Pulver by happenstance.

One of my closest friends, Kevin Jandt, invited me to a men's group at a local gym. The genesis of the gathering was to create a forum where men could discuss a book called *The Purpose Driven Life*. Each week we reviewed a chapter and its contents, debating how author Rick Warren's words related to our own lives. Our attempt was to become better people and grow spiritually, a particularly tall order for some of us. The small group concept was not terribly original or unique; however, this setting was far from ordinary. You see, this gym was not your garden variety workout facility. It was comprised of the toughest men on the planet, literally. Per square foot, this building produced more sweat, blood, and suffering than almost any place on earth.

I wasn't one of the founding four members of the group but joined early, and the attendees now numbered six. At first, the gathering was so quaint that we met in a small office, assembled five or six nonmatching chairs, and sat in a broken circle. The room had two large desks, papers, and boxes strewn across the floor; various pictures decorated the walls. As you looked at the cast of characters, it was a mishmash of age, experiences, and demographics. Even with only a few men in the room, the individualism was staggering, making the experience uncommonly unique, engaging, stirring, and real. Few things in life are truly real. This fellowship was real.

As I soaked in this weekly encounter, I was convinced that we had something special here; once people discovered it, perhaps it could change the world. I am not exaggerating or being flippant. I believed we could change the world, one guy at a time.

The roster consisted of the following cast of hombres:

The spiritual leader of our session was Keith, the youth pastor of the church that Kevin and I attended. Keith had jet-black hair and typically wore a T-shirt that doubled as a message board. Phrases he donned included Obey, Trust, Affliction, or Submit, just to name a few. Years back, he was the drummer in a rock band. Although drumming is his specialty, he is an exceptional guitar player and vocalist as well. His musical acumen was so abundant it actually annoyed the rest of us. Just after the band released its first album, he felt his spirit called to the ministry, prayed about what to do, then promptly dropped everything and moved to Davenport, Iowa. Remember the T-shirts. He ain't kidding. At thirty, second youngest in the group, he had more leadership and discernment talents than the rest of us combined. Therefore, without an official ceremony, he was anointed the de facto chairman of the board.

George, founding member of the group, was a sixty-three-year-old business owner who became our elder statesman.

Standing six feet four, most of his white hair intact, he was as skinny as a rail. George played basketball for the University of Iowa in the mid-1950s and had flown helicopters in the army and national guard. Currently, he owned a successful machine shop in town and was clearly a born leader. George possessed a type A personality and businesslike approach to most subjects. You could tell that he was accustomed to calling the shots and getting results. We learned quickly that George had elevated to professional status, with regard to giving people second chances. In fact, the person running his multimillion dollar enterprise was a hitchhiker he picked up thirty years before.

Kevin occupied the next chair in the room. He, along with George, was responsible for getting the group off the ground. A former college wrestler turned stud triathlete, Kevin is as tough as they come. Yet, what is so amazing and cool about this guy is that he can quickly navigate into a thoughtful, spiritual juggernaut. Another one of his talents is that he can provide superior advice on how to handle the most difficult situations. Kevin is a relatively quiet guy, yet one should never underestimate him in terms of passion or competitiveness. When roused, he will show a fire that is not easily extinguished.

It is often said that relationships are cemented when you experience suffering together. Kevin and I were training partners for an Ironman Triathlon. This event combines a 2.4 mile swim, 112 mile bike and 26.2 mile run, all in a single day. As you tread water, with twenty-five hundred other athletes at the virtual starting line, you have been told there is only a single guarantee that day: you will suffer. If you finish the journey and meet your goals, consider it a bonus. We trained for fifty-two weeks straight, side by side, for thousands of miles. We did it all together: the physical and mental agony, highs and lows, improvements and setbacks. Unplanned and miraculously, we finished the 140.6 mile endeavor just three seconds apart. Kevin is the big brother that I never had.

Sitting next to Kevin was the youngest member of the group, a kid named Anthony. He was a twenty-three-year-old who had recently returned from the military conflict in Iraq, wise beyond his years and with a special appreciation for life. On more than one occasion, a mortar round fired by the insurgent movement landed within feet of where he was standing. He will inform you, with relative calm, that he shouldn't be alive today. These explosives should have detonated, should have killed him and his comrades.

Anthony's quiet composure is countered by a razor sharp opinion on most issues. He is unwavering on many beliefs and won't back down to anyone. If regarding a topic he held dear, there was absolutely no wiggle room with him. The characteristic conveyed a certain level of security for those who considered this man their friend.

To my left, the fourth original member was a man named Pat Miletich. I would need an entire book to list this man's résumé. Pat Miletich is a living legend. He is iconic, a five-time world champion in MMA, with black belts in karate and jujitsu. He owns a United States Muay Thai kickboxing title and has an undefeated record in professional boxing. In addition, he has trained the most accomplished athletes in the sport. Miletich leads and teaches the most well-known, well-respected camp in the industry, with affiliate schools throughout North America.

It is wildly believed that Pat Miletich has trained more world champions in MMA than any other individual on the planet. Lastly, regardless of the city or state, when law enforcement, police, or security forces need self-defense training, Pat Miletich is often the first guy they call.

His life has been followed and chronicled for many years, and, even as I write, the television show *60 Minutes* is doing a story on him. However, if you are fortunate enough to know Pat as a friend, you are impressed with something far different from what you might expect. Substantially more amazing than his exhaustive list of physical accomplishments is his pure heart. Pat is simply a decent man. He redefines the qualities of selflessness and generosity. Pat responsibly possesses an endless supply of credibility with impressionable and sometimes troubled men. He utilizes this as currency to teach, mentor, and change lives.

The first time I met him, I knew I liked him. It was that easy. In one of the first Wednesday groups I attended, he eloquently explained his philosophy regarding his team. Here is one of the toughest guys on earth, instilling in his team that "fighting may be what we do, but it's not who we are."

I rounded out the group. The best way to describe myself is to say I'm a futurist, confused by the contemporary world. However, I had crystal clarity on one subject: my group. These were my brothers. And now, this was my most sacred hour of each week. Deep down, I believed this motley crew would change the world.

Our weekly encounters had flourished in terms of quality and depth. Keith would unpack the topic of the week and somehow make each of us believe that Rick Warren wrote the book for us, individually. Kevin and I would come away each week wondering how the experience could possibly become better, but it did. Each assembly seemed to be more amazing than the last. A few more guys would trickle in, yet few would achieve frequent-flier status. For about four months, the number of attendees toggled between five and nine.

Looking back, there were a few sessions that seemed to change the destiny of the group. Perhaps it was the topic of the day. Perhaps it was a spirited discussion. And sometimes it was a person's stirring testimony about finding God and changing his life for eternity.

The Wednesday group originally met in this small office.

Now, some meetings have over thirty-five attendees.

Square Jaw

Although I had been making the trek to Pat's gym for many consecutive Wednesdays, I was still a neophyte in terms of Mixed Martial Arts knowledge and the men who trained there. At one particular session, an engaging thirty-something guy, with a square jaw and particularly impressive build, joined us for the day. He sat on the floor, covered in sweat—bare feet, workout pants, and a gray-and-black T-shirt. At first glance, his shirt seemed to be promoting the army or some other branch of the United States military. The bold black letters, I thought, said, "Army of One."

Today's session was especially riveting, and most everyone had something to say, including the man whom I had never met. Although his discussion insight was above average, I couldn't shake the fact his neck circumference dwarfed my waistline. After the session, Kevin pulled me aside and asked, "Do you know who that cat was?"

"Nope," I said. "The only thing I know is that he's built like a brick sh-t house." Kevin informed me it was Matt Hughes, the reigning 170-pound world champion in the UFC (Ultimate Fighting Championship). He was considered the most dominant figure in the entire league. Not simply a champion but the most feared, complete, and well-respected athlete in the sport.

Furthermore, Kevin advised me his T-shirt said "Army of *the* One" (emphasis added). What a difference a single word can make. Matt's shirt was proclaiming his faith as a Christian. As I played back some of the stories Matt talked about in the gathering, I was beginning to appreciate him even more. In an industry where toughness, bravado, ego, and even nastiness reign supreme, Matt was eloquent, thoughtful, and endearing.

Matt explained to us that, a couple of years ago, he and his twin brother, Mark, went on a missionary trip to Central America, an orphanage called Rancho 3 M. It was during this experience that Matt was introduced to a painting entitled "Who Cares." The picture consisted of perhaps two dozen people on a platform out at sea. Although their foundation appeared steady, the waters surrounding them were raging and tumultuous; crashing waves filled the scene.

The individuals were performing routine functions such as talking on phones—some sitting, others standing, one guy playing a guitar, and another calmly casting a fishing rod and reel. However, these mundane, common acts were contrasted against an equal number of people who had fallen into the water. Most were desperate, all were struggling, and drowning appeared imminent to each and every person.

Matt decided to place himself in the picture and ask the introspective question, "Who would I be?" He looked deep inside and determined, although he wasn't pleased with the answer, no doubt about it, he would be drowning. Matt had always held a deep respect and admiration for his brother. However, Mark's recent decision to accept Jesus Christ as his personal Lord and Savior had particularly inspired Matt. Perhaps Mark felt it was just the right moment; he had his brother's undivided attention, so he turned to him and issued a few simple words: "The time is now."

That night, Matt experienced what he could best describe as an epiphany. Suddenly and unexpectedly, his life took on new direction. Past mistakes were washed clean, and forgiveness replaced guilt. Sometimes, when people refer to their faith journey, you will hear references to "getting out of the boat."

Matt Hughes was out of the boat.

The next day, I visited the gym and noticed Matt in the weight room. He was training for an upcoming fight in Las Vegas where he would defend his title against Joe Riggs, a formidable up-and-comer. Only a few days later, Anthony, George, Kevin, Keith, and I started discussing a trip to watch him compete. Although this was totally extemporaneous, it seemed like a completely workable plan: fly up the day of the event and return the next morning. We would support Matt and gain another opportunity for fellowship. I wondered if I was the only one who could fully appreciate the lunacy of what was ahead. Someone once told me that "crazy people are the last to know they're crazy," which caused me a great deal of personal consternation. It strikes me as curious that a youth pastor, a twenty-something war veteran, a triathlete/chip timer, an obsessive-compulsive executive, and some guy knocking at the eligibility door of Social Security would load up, scurry off to Sin City, and observe grown men legally punch each other.

Within days of the initial psychosis, we purchased our tickets, and the plan was born.

Matt Hughes getting ready for practice at Pat's gym.

Pack Your Bags

The trek to Las Vegas was a few weeks away. I thought it would be prudent to discuss the details with my wife, Michelle. On a Saturday morning, as habit would have it, we headed to Starbucks for a cup of mud. I preferred the venti Verona (room for cream), and she would order some holistic green-tea concoction. On the way, Michelle called her friend Krista Rittenhouse and proceeded to brief her on my insanity, mentioning I would be heading to Vegas for a UFC event.

Krista was aware that I had been attending the group at Pat's gym and asked Michelle if I knew of a certain guy that trained down there. As we approached Starbucks, my five-year-old son, Steele, and two-year-old daughter, Macey Marie, were chirping in the middle bay of the SUV. Hence, I could only hear about 20 percent of what Michelle was asking me.

"Do you know a guy named [unintelligible]?" she inquired.

I responded, "Who? What's his name?"

Michelle went on: "I think Krista said Jens something."

"Jens? Jens who?" I questioned.

"Jens Pulver," she answered.

"No, I have never heard of him," I responded. "Who is he, and how does Krista know him?"

Krista mentioned to Michelle that her husband, Todd, had been praying for this guy, every single day for nearly four years. I was blown away. It was a good day if I could pray for someone for five seconds before becoming distracted. Every day for four years, now that's impressive. Todd was the kind of individual that doesn't give up easily. If he had been on his knees for this guy, day after day, I determined there must be something extraordinary about the commitment.

As the next couple of weeks passed, the anticipation of our trip grew. It was a much-needed shift from the daily grind. As we discussed our preparations for the journey, our checklists varied widely. Keith had a few eateries on his hit list. George was scouring the internet for churches. Kevin was mapping out a running course for the two of us. Anthony was simply pleased we were staying in a hotel, as he was accustomed to a cot in the Iraqi desert. Although I didn't disclose my secret, I was investigating the spa services at the MGM Grand. If men are truly honest with themselves, deep inside of every male psyche is the longing for a hot-stone massage with Aveda-inspired scented oils.

The morning finally arrived, and our trek included an eighty-minute drive from the Quad Cities to Peoria, followed by a nonstop flight to Las Vegas. Kevin was kind enough to offer his large, late-model pickup to transport the fivesome. He was quite proud of his vehicle, particularly its appearance. I sent out an APB to the rest of the guys that, if anyone spilled a beverage or drooled on the arm rest, just cover it up and keep quiet. We didn't need Mr. Clean busting anyone's chops at 5:00 AM.

The check-in at the airport went seamlessly, almost. After my comrades skated through the process unimpeded, I got the Homeland Security smack-down. Normally a freak regarding attention to detail, I failed miserably that day. My driver's license had expired six months earlier, and I had no other form of picture identification. I felt a bead of sweat running down the back of my neck as the skeptics behind the counter sized me up and down. As it turned out, they asked me to step into the "special" corral and simply placed the infamous black wand in places where investigation shouldn't be necessary. After receiving exactly four "you idiot" looks, I sheepishly proceeded to the ticket gate. Within an hour, wheels were up.

The flight was uneventful with respect to turbulence or power failures. My goal was to read a book and relax, but I couldn't help myself. I had three or four hours with Keith and knew he couldn't run away, even if he wanted to. In the previous two years of my life, I repeatedly made poor decisions, jumped the tracks, and screwed up my life a bit. For thirty-four years, I had accumulated a squeaky clean report card, then unexpectedly was having trouble getting the "Thou shalt not" list right.

One of my conversational motives was to ask Keith if God was accepting of damaged and broken goods. I picked his brain on topics of Christianity, faith, and forgiveness, trying to ascertain if he was interested in the chatter or felt like it was his day off as a pastor and just wanted to close his eyes. If he was annoyed, he didn't let on and graciously answered my questions with unimaginable insight. As we descended through the clouds, I was reminded of how fortunate I was to have these friends.

Our bird was now on the tarmac and slowly approached the offloading gate. We disembarked, found the baggage claim, and obtained the small amount of luggage we had previously deemed necessary. Then we marched toward the closest exit sign to hail a cab, or so I thought. As I mentioned earlier, George was comfortable making group decisions. He determined that twenty-five dollars for a ride to the hotel was tantamount to financial persecution, and we would be walking to our destination.

The MGM Grand was a mile or two away; with elementary arithmetic, I felt compelled to state the obvious: the cab fare was only five dollars per man. Kevin, the consummate diplomat, advised me not to be disruptive to team unity and instructed me to go with the flow. As we ambled through what appeared to be restricted areas of the airport property, I pictured TSA officials in security towers proclaiming, "What in the hell are these clowns doing? Someone please shoot them."

I wasn't terribly concerned with the distance of the hike. After all, Kevin and I would regularly record weeks of fifty-plus miles of running. For some reason, I just felt it was ludicrous. Notwithstanding my mental struggles, we soon arrived at our hotel.

From a Distance

Within minutes of checking in, we found ourselves bumping into the who's who of the UFC. Ten feet from us was Joe Rogan, host of the TV series *Fear Factor*. Joe was the co-announcer of the production and the voice that millions would hear that night, broadcast through an enormous pay-per-view audience. We looked down the massive entrance area to see Andrei Arlovski chatting into his cell phone. Andre held the heavyweight title belt and resembled a gigantic vampire. I'm not positive, but as I watched him converse, it actually appeared he had fangs.

By now, I could see rows of slot machines and hordes of people, and I smelled the displeasing fragrance of cigarettes. Keith and I strolled deeper into the hotel and made a right turn. Flash bulbs were popping, blazing, and igniting as we traveled down the hallway in anticipation. The attraction was Joe Riggs, the opponent of our guy, Matt Hughes. His hands were raised in the familiar fight stance, and I could see he loved the attention. I felt a bizarre animosity toward him. This feeling was unjustified since I had never met the fellow, and he hadn't done anything malevolent to me personally. Perhaps it was more that I felt loyalty to Matt, rather than disliking Joe. However, later that night, he would be attempting to dethrone our Miletich man and take his title. I just couldn't bring myself to be fond of him.

Anthony's stomach was rumbling, and Keith had exhausted the calories from the PowerBar I gave him earlier. George recommended we eat at the restaurant on the main floor and there were no objections. We experienced virtually no delay and were seated promptly. If you scanned the room, you noticed an enormous amount of diversity. In addition, tattoos per capita were above the national average. I happen to appreciate ink, having a fair share of my own, so I admired the artwork. Just before my grilled chicken breast with Dijon mustard showed up, a group of fellows sauntered by our table. Immediately, you knew what these guys did for a living; they were fighters. I was sitting next to Kevin when he informed me, "That's Jens Pulver."

I replied, "Unbelievable. That's the same guy my buddy Todd has been praying for, every night for four years. How do you know him?"

Kevin responded, "I met him at the gym and talked to him a couple of times. Arguably, he is the most exciting competitor in the UFC. He faced unbelievable abuse while he was growing up and somehow managed to survive. If you were to know a fraction of what he endured at the hands of his father, you would vomit."

For the entire lunch, I pondered the words that Kevin uttered and watched Jens across the room, from a distance. I couldn't help but think of my own son, Steele, and wonder how someone could hurt a child, his own child. It obviously wasn't the first time I heard of maltreatment, yet it was different this time. Usually, I would become sad at this sort of news; this time, I got freaking pissed off. If you're going to raise your fists to strike someone, put on the gloves, size up, and throw hands. Just don't hit a kid, damn it, don't hit a kid. That just pissed me off.

In my mind, for whatever reason, I had pictured Jens as a massive, colossal figure. I miscalculated. My first guess would put him at five feet eight in height and maybe 165 pounds. He had a muscular build, full head of dark brown hair, and the look of a rough, no-question-about-it, crazy-tough fighter. The guys knew most of his friends at the table, all credible names in the world of MMA. "Ruthless" Robbie Lawler, Ben Uker, and boxing specialist Matt Pena flanked Jens. We surmised it was the safest table in the building. My next thought was simple: how do I get this guy to attend the Wednesday group? This thought became incessant for the rest of the day.

After lunch, we spent the next few hours walking the strip and purchasing the obligatory trinkets for the family. There is nothing that quite says I love you like cheap, Chinese-made souvenirs. The sidewalk trek also included the unrelenting bombardment of pornographic collateral. Every ten feet of our journey, we were approached by non-English speaking men with baseball-card-size pictures of naked women. These were presumably either for night clubs or escort services, and it appeared their supply was endless.

The scenery also included a deranged preacher on a milk crate, damning the nearest passerby to hell; others with the unoriginal idea of dressing up like Elvis; tattoos galore; and people brandishing pierced body parts that I didn't know a piercing gun could locate. I couldn't help but think of how dissimilar this was from my life in Bettendorf, Iowa. Within moments of my daydream, the MGM Grand was in sight and the main event was only a few short hours away.

The tribe decided to head back to the hotel room and relax for a couple of hours. Just as Anthony grabbed the remote to engage in channel surfing, I created some lame excuse—like, I was going to see where the ice machine was located—when, in actuality, my massage appointment was starting in ten minutes, and I needed to invent a getaway plan. In rather innocuous fashion, I slipped out the door and strolled to the nearest elevator. After signing in, I was given a robe with above-average qualities in terms of softness and comfort. Since I didn't know anyone in the waiting area, and wasn't particularly interested in small talk, I grabbed a fitness magazine and kept to myself.

Minutes later, my name was called and off I went. The massage was decent but nothing to write home about. The only extraordinary characteristic about the experience was the inflated price tag. Back in the men's locker room, I put my original garb back on and contemplated how I was going to explain my absence. The guys would surely blow through the ice machine story. As I entered the hotel room, I enlightened my friends that I needed to come out of the closet; I admitted that I was metrosexual. Shopping at Express for Men, spa treatments, and shaving my legs (cycling) were all current addictions. I made no apologies, and my buddies accepted me with open arms and a warm understanding of the truth. It was a liberating experience for all of us.

Our nap time had expired, and it was time to grab a quick bite to eat and make our way to the event. By now, the excitement and anticipation were building. We headed to the arena to locate our seats. Matt Hughes had secured the tickets for us, and we were grateful for his help. As we stood in line and proceeded through the herd of people, we all realized this was a pretty big deal. The sport was exploding in terms of notoriety and exposure: thousands upon thousands of people flooded through the doors to the stadium. As we took our seats, we were all extremely energized. We couldn't wait to watch Matt compete.

The bouts that preceded Matt's fight were respectable and orderly, yet my concentration was spotty. Although our surroundings were noisy and raucous, I was thinking about our Wednesday group most of the time. I was also thinking about Jens. I wanted him to know the guys. I wanted him to get a taste of our fellowship. As I snapped back into my current reality, the lights in the arena had been turned off, and I realized that Matt was next on the card. Riggs came out first and danced around the octagon, and then the lights turned off again. The song "Country Boy Can Survive," by Hank Williams Jr., blared through the sound system as he steadily made his way into the ring.

Matt was so calm, it was eerie. He just slowly paced back and forth, glaring over at his opponent. Without saying a word, the message was, "You have picked the wrong guy—so beware."

As the match started, we were on the edge of our seats; anything can happen in these contests. In a workmanlike fashion, Matt simply took him down and imposed his will. He grabbed his arm, twisting it into a Kimura submission technique, and Riggs tapped out. It was over within a minute or two of the first round. We flew out of our seats and managed to display a few aggressive fist pumps.

"That a boy, Matt, that a boy!" we screamed.

Then one of the guys, I can't remember who, said, "Sh-t, man, that was quick."

After viewing one more quick clash that night, we marched back to our rooms and crashed.

The next morning, after grabbing my Starbucks bold brew, I joined the team for breakfast. Although buffets are typically on my "no chance in hell" list, I made an exception. I have to admit there was an amazing spread, and we made an admirable dent in the hotel's offering. Once we had consumed twice what we needed for daily survival, we called a cab and headed off to church.

The service was decent, and the congregation was extremely friendly to us. In fact, so friendly that George figured someone would likely give us a ride back to the hotel. Apparently, if the mission succeeded, we were going to collectively save a total of eleven dollars. As Kevin, Anthony, Keith, and I waited outside, George combed through the crowd for a willing participant. He was unsuccessful in his first several attempts but then appeared to land a contestant. Some guy named Roy or Bob or Frank—I can't remember—indicated that it would be his pleasure to take us back to the MGM Grand. I just remember he had a mustache and looked to be about forty-five years old.

The car was a beige, two-door coupe, which could comfortably accommodate four adults. On a good day, five smaller people might squeeze in, if necessary. Since George stood six feet four, he peeled back the front passenger seat and invited us to cram into the backseat. As the four of us sandwiched into the back, unfortunately I settled into the right middle slot. I had about 15 percent of one butt cheek on the seat, and my knees were touching my chin. To add to the chaos, the driver was a miserable chauffer. He would toggle between neck-jolting braking and abrupt accelerations. Since it was ninety degrees inside the vehicle, and oxygen was at a premium, I asked him to either roll down the windows or turn on the air-conditioning. He looked confused as he scrambled to find the necessary buttons and controls to honor my request. As he slammed on the brakes for the tenth time, I leaned over to Anthony and said, "This isn't even this cat's car."

Within seconds, a confession emerged: "Frank" stated, "Hey, guys, I don't own a car; I borrowed this from a member at church."

At that point, I freaked out. "Listen up, jokers; this is the last time I'm going to deal with this crap. We are taking a cab to the airport. I'll pay for the whole damn cost if necessary. I'm not walking. I'm not riding on a luggage cart. I'm not renting a skateboard. I'm taking a freaking cab to the airport. Any questions, you clowns?"

To my utter delight, no one wanted to brawl. As abstract as it may have sounded, we agreed to procure a taxi for the ride.

Within several hours and, thankfully, seamless boarding procedures, our plane was airborne. At thirty-three thousand feet, you have time to ponder. As I nervously hoped the boys at Boeing had placed every wing rivet properly, I again began to forecast how we would manage to ensure Jens would attend our next meeting. I learned others had invited him countless times, and countless times he was a no-show. So it was time to up the ante and bring in a hired gun. My choice was easy: I would employ the talents of Kevin Jandt.

During our preparation for Ironman, my fellow training partners dubbed Kevin "T3". I don't know why athletes often give each other mindless, freshman nicknames; but we do. Kevin's alter ego was derived from the fact that he was the last of us to ever tap out. It didn't matter if we were in the pool, on the bike, or logging running miles, he would never give up. He became almost an android during his workouts.

There were days where the temperature was well below zero, winds whipping us up and down, ice on the ground, an eighteen-mile run ahead of us, and someone would encourage the group to abbreviate the agony. Our routes often included strategically placed coffee shops. It would be so easy to just stop, take a break, and enjoy some dark, hot, liquid heaven. Despite knowing the answer in advance, we continued to test the waters. On no account whatsoever would Kevin take a shortcut. We would hear him chant repeatedly, "Must run longer; must not stop; must go on."

When it comes to bringing people to Jesus, Kevin had a definite, enviable persistence about his methods. He wasn't overbearing, obnoxious, or pushy; he just delicately balanced nudging with opportunity. It was about ten months and a dozen or so invitations before I attended Kevin's church. Since the first experience, my family rarely misses a week. We had gone over a decade without attending church, and now can't wait to get there. I remain indebted to him for his persistence.

It was now a few weeks after our Vegas trip, and the group was noticeably larger, maybe a dozen or more men. According to standard operating procedure, we began to gather our chairs and create our modified circle. The seats were now emerging from various locations of the gym. The most coveted chairs were the gray, cushioned ones, which were borrowed from the front desk area and carried upstairs. There were two wicker units we commandeered from the massage waiting room and several cafeteria-style folding units from cardio land. The least desirable options were the black, plastic chairs from the wrestling room. These bad boys were utilized to rest between rounds of boxing, grappling, or pounding of the heavy bags. If you were lucky enough to end up with one of these gems, you couldn't help but inherit bodily fluids from the previous occupant, whether you were planning on it or not.

In the midst of my preoccupation to avoid a "black nasty," I noticed a first-timer ascending the stairs. Despite uncountable predictions that this would never happen, and to the disbelief of everyone in attendance, there was a quiet respectfulness that blanketed the room: heads turned gently as Jens Pulver joined the group.

Jens enjoys a moment of peace.

The First Step

Although we didn't communicate the thought with words, Keith, Kevin, Pat, and I understood this would be an important day. Many Wednesdays before, we were told that Jens would be attending; yet his chair remained vacant. We would later learn that he often left minutes before commencement, traveled the short distance to his residence, and went on lockdown. He would shut the door to his room, batten down the hatches, and, more importantly, block out the outside world.

Jens actually didn't even plan on attending this session but, rather, was headed to the chiropractic clinic. As he finished the stair climb, he found himself walking right through the middle of fifteen men who had assembled. He felt a calmness and peace about the decision to simply sit down.

Jens told me later that he felt God had been whispering to him as he looked at us: "It's time for you to take a seat, and it's time for you to trust."

He didn't know our names. He didn't know our stories. He didn't know our brokenness, triumphs, or character. He didn't know our failings. Without knowing more than three attendees, and having never been there before, Jens recognized it was safe. It was safe to be exposed. It was safe to be vulnerable. It was safe to let go. He had nothing more than the nakedness of blind faith but knew it would be different. He knew he had brothers. In less than two minutes, Jens Pulver had fifteen new brothers.

In what I would later learn to be a patented, nonconforming move, Jens avoided the four existing chair options and grabbed a large, blue, core-workout ball to sit on. For the first several minutes of the session, his eyes focused mainly down and straight ahead, as he bounced ever so gently on his three-foot-wide spherical chair. I couldn't determine if he was engaged in Keith's words or spent the time repeating to himself, "What in the hell am I doing here?"

To the surprise of many, Jens introduced himself and began speaking openly and with reckless abandon. Before he completed the first few sentences, his delivery included thought-gathering pauses, tears, somberness, and bravery— plenty of bravery. He indicated that, once again, he had been battling limitless demons. He was tired, beat up, mentally and physically drained, just flat angry. I glanced around the room and noticed the guys were frozen. They were in a trance. Every single person was staring directly at him, mesmerized with his words. Jens went on to inform us he had a heavy chest, felt enormous guilt for being away from his family, missed his mother and little brother, and still harbored extreme resentment for his father. All those years of abuse, self-doubt, and pain constantly swirled in his head. His brother Dustin, who had been recently and infamously featured on the television show *America's Most Wanted*, had just been captured. Dustin would face life in prison, with no chance of parole.

Other than that, he smiled, life was perfect.

Jens went on to say he didn't particularly like groups and, in the past, people had advised him he wasn't quite good enough for this type of setting. Whether it was a traditional church, consisting of bricks and mortar, or a nontraditional venue like the Wednesday group, he was told his pedigree didn't quite qualify. He was also dumbfounded that it cost money to go to church. He piped in with color: "Sh-t, man, I couldn't believe it when they told me you have to bring cash and drop it in the bucket. I'm not the brightest guy in the world, but I didn't know God was short on funds." He finished, "What the hell is that noise? So what if you don't have any money? Did that mean you weren't welcome?"

Even though we had only known him for thirty-six minutes, there was just something incredibly intoxicating about Jens Pulver. The first thing I kept thinking to myself was how real he was. He was so damn genuine that you almost couldn't stand it. Most of us were not accustomed to this sort of individual. Some of the rest of us were still wearing our masks, conforming to the pressures and rituals of the outside world. We had to dress a certain way, talk a certain way, and act a certain way. It's so much work. It's so exhausting. It takes so much effort. When you're worried about what everyone else thinks, you begin to transform into the person wearing the mask, almost forgetting about or refusing to acknowledge who you are inside.

This was not an issue for Jens. What you saw was what you got. And, by the way, if you didn't like what you saw, don't expect an apology. It wasn't forthcoming. To the contrary, it would be considered a mistake to approach Jens and offer the following incredulous advice: "Excuse me, Mr. Pulver, I was stirred today by your testimony; however, it occurred to me that you used eleven curse words during your delivery. I also noticed your shirt has a rip in it and may even contain a ketchup stain from a rogue cheeseburger. Might I recommend it would be in your best interest to consider revising your noun-verb structure and taking your shirt to the dry cleaners. I believe then, and only then, will your story be considered credible and convincing."

If, by some rare and unfortunate chance, you made that mistake, then I would pray for mercy on your soul. You would likely wake up in your underwear, lying on a table in a sterile, stark, white room, with bright lights and several strangers. As your eyes focused, you would smell the distinct bouquet of antiseptic products and see rubber-glove dispensers everywhere. After you determined what hospital you had been transported to, you would seek out a mirror to survey the damage and notice you were now donning new headgear, in the form of one of those erector-set-type cranium braces. Its sole function would be to carefully keep proper tension and stability on your newly fractured skull. So, if you ever feel a compulsive urge to pontificate your unsolicited wisdom on your neighbor, make sure you don't live next door to Jens. Rule number one: don't lecture Jens Pulver.

After our gathering adjourned, everyone stood and went through our ritual of handshakes, knuckle bumps, and "See you next Wednesday" statements. This day was different. When Jens spoke, many of us were blown off our chairs. It was as if we had just returned from a speeding rollercoaster for the first time. As the harness tension is released and raised, you disembark from the ride. Your heart is pounding, and the force of the experience is still with you. Your legs are a bit wobbly as you make your way to the exit area.

A number of guys walked up to Jens and shook his hand. They expressed how grateful they were for his honesty. Here was one of the toughest guys in the world, allowing others to see his struggles. He trusted us enough for our input, and we took the responsibility seriously. As I made it through the receiving line and approached Jens, I extended my hand and said, "Jens, my name is Tim, and you belong in this group."

He looked at me with a certain level of thankfulness and replied, "I think you're right."

As the weeks passed, Jens had come to the group several times and seemed to enjoy this hour on Wednesday. Yet, as with many new endeavors, after a person gains traction, it's sometimes difficult to stay with the program. His attendance was spotty for the next many weeks; then, without notice, he essentially disappeared, without a trace. About a month and a half had passed, and no one knew why he vanished. The only thing we knew was that the answer might be more elusive than finding Jens himself.

Jesus said that wherever two or more are gathered in his name, he is present. Therefore, the number of attendees was never the driving force for the session to be valid or rewarding. Admittedly, however, there was an added element of spice whenever Jens was there. Perhaps it was his unpredictability; perhaps it was the way he told a story; perhaps it was the lump in your throat when he bared his soul. Whatever it was, it was different, and it was riveting.

Although Kevin and I had begun our friendship with Jens, it was still in the infancy stages. Trust in a relationship is paramount to Jens; not many things are more important to him. Few people knew this kid better than his manager, Monte Cox, and coach, Pat Miletich. Jens has told me countless times that coaches raised him. From the age of nine all the way through his college days, he had one mentor after the other. These men, each different and each illustrating unique lessons for Jens, have shaped him into the person he is today. His fourth-grade wrestling coach was Jack Vantrass. As he entered fifth and sixth grades, it was Lang Davidson. Junior high brought the talents of Russ Hayden, and in high school it was Brian Higa. Two brothers, Dan and Randy Staab, were with Jens from seventh through twelfth grade. At Boise State College, he was tutored by head coach Mike Young and assistant coaches Greg Randall and Chris Owens.

In a way, these men were surrogate fathers for Jens. At different points in his life, always with impeccable timing, he would make the transition from one amazing mentor to the next. They provided counsel, structure, encouragement, love, and support, shaping him during his most impressionable years. If anyone knew where he had gone, what struggles he was facing, or if he would ever return to the group, Monte Cox and Pat Miletich would. To understand how these friendships emerged, you need to rewind the clock about seven years.

Jens and his chair of preference at the Wednesday group.

Keith leads the Wednesday group with an opening prayer.

The Full Monte

It is fully exposed, raw, and naked. There is nothing left for the mind's imagination. The friendship between Jens and his manager is in full view, for everyone to see. Their rich and trusting relationship has a deep, profound history. Over many years, they have forged a bond that cannot be penetrated or dismantled.

In the early part of 2000, Jens and a friend named Nate Petit were traveling to Jens's first UFC event in Lake Charles, Louisiana. At the time, there was no pay-per-view or cable audience, and the sport was only legal in about three states. To the shock and dismay of most Americans, Louisiana was on the short list of acceptable venues.

Nate was actually the reason that Jens began a career in MMA. The first time they met was during a training session. Shortly after a brief introduction, they were paired up and began wrestling and sparring. Nate delivered a kick to the side of Jens's leg that he will never forget. "When that kick landed, I saw stars. I had never felt pain like that before," Jens recalled. "I wanted to find out more about his kickboxing skills and learn these techniques."

After Nate witnessed Jens's wrestling prowess, he came to a quick conclusion. He envisioned that if Jens combined his wrestling background with kickboxing, grappling, and boxing, he could be unstoppable. Inside of one training session, he saw the pure talent that Jens possessed. He saw something special. He saw that Jens could be great.

The flight itinerary included a stop in the Houston airport before a final destination of Lake Charles. As luck would have it, there were significant delays and backlogged flights. Jens became slightly annoyed at this news; however, he didn't have other options. As he and Nate found a way to pass the time, a few traveling outlaws approached the waiting area. Although he didn't know any of their names at the time, the group consisted of: Monte Cox, Pat Miletich, Matt Hughes, and Jeremy Horn.

Nate and Pat actually knew each other. Nate had been a student of Pat's in previous kickboxing classes. Brief pleasantries were exchanged, and the gang hung out together in the area near the ticket gate. As the intercom voice rang with more irritating news, the group determined the chance for a flight out of Houston was fading fast. They were informed there may be a single plane leaving; however, that flight had more passengers than seats.

Even though they had met only hours before, Monte and Pat offered to give up their seat assignments. They informed Jens and Nate that, if anyone was going to Lake Charles, it would be them. Jens was dumbfounded. A random act of kindness from a virtual stranger—something didn't smell right. Yet there were no hidden agendas, none at all. As it turned out, everyone boarded the plane and made the safe trip to Louisiana. Before the fortunate turn of events, Monte and Pat had sacrificed their weekend. They traded their agenda for the chance that Jens might shine.

Monte told me he liked Jens the moment they met. "I just remember meeting this kid and he was smiling all the time. He was so excited to receive this opportunity. We ended up spending time in the same locker room on the night of the event. After he won the fight, I got a chance to speak with him; he was on the top of the world."

What happened next was extremely rare and confusing. Although Jens had his hand raised in the ring, as the plain and unmistakable winner, officials came back to the locker room and changed the decision. They made the determination the bout would be ruled a draw.

Jens felt powerless, devastated, and robbed. His victory, barely minutes old, had been seized. Monte carefully watched Jens absorb the news and summon the courage to deal with this travesty. What he witnessed amazed him: Jens's character and how he handled adversity. He wondered how a youngster could be so accomplished and graceful at handling this appalling verdict. Monte, like so many people who meet Jens, saw that he was extraordinary. Although you can't quite put your finger on why you know, you are positive that Jens Pulver is special.

Monte received a phone call from legendary trainer Bob Shamrock shortly after returning home from Louisiana. Bob was the father of Ken Shamrock who, because of his strength, talent, and reputation, had been dubbed "the most dangerous man alive." Bob was running a camp called Shamrock 2000 and wanted to know if Monte had room for one of his fighters. He indicated there was a gifted athlete that needed a stable of training partners to fully realize his potential. The future of Shamrock 2000 was in question, and he felt this youngster would be better served by sending him to Bettendorf. Monte replied, "I may have room for him; what's his name?" Bob said the name was Jens Pulver. Monte smiled. "I know that kid; send him my way."

Meanwhile, back in Boise, Idaho, Jens was contemplating which camp he would call home. He was immensely thankful to Bob and, at the same time, knew he needed to make a change. As skillful as his current wrestling team was, as great as the boxing team he had in his camp, he knew he had to be with fighters. Nate continued advising Jens that relocating, although difficult, was also necessary. Jens recalled, "Nate had more faith in me than I did. He had the vision and knew the destination. He told me to pack my sh-t up and hop a train."

Leaving would not be easy, but world champions aren't man-ufactured easily. If he was going to be the best in the world, the decision of where to train became obvious. Jens would need to be at the Miletich camp.

Two days later, Jens arrived at Galesburg, Illinois; he exited the train with a duffle bag in each hand: one stocked with workout gear, the other plain street clothes. Jammed in the remaining vacancy of the bags were about two and a half days' worth of food rations and a bag of quarters from his mother.

Monte picked him up at the station and drove him to the Quad Cities. The duo of Monte and Pat would also ensure that Jens would land softly in his new environment. Since Jens did not have a place to stay, Monte took care of that small detail. He allowed Jens to stay at his house. Never mind that Monte already had an established family unit, with a wife and two girls. Jens needed a break, and Monte didn't blink.

Monte looks back: "When you live with a guy for three months, you pretty much know everything about him. Jens grows on you [pause] like a fungus."

After Monte chuckles in his chair, he goes on to say, "It is what it is; some people just click. I was impressed with Jens from the start. He's always got a smile, and we just make each other laugh. I'm not only his manager; we are the best of friends. He doesn't know it yet, but I'm going to have him follow my girls around when they start dating."

Monte's smile fades, and he speaks in a sober, humorless tone: "Their boyfriends don't have a chance."

Never

Monte and I finish our conversation by speaking about the loyalty among Pat, Jens, and himself. "Two things come to mind," Monte says. "The three of us have always had a connection; and, now that I think of it, Pat and I are the only ones that will put up with his sh-t."

Monte and Jens

There Is No "I" in Miletich

Once in town, there were occasions where Pat picked up Jens and drove him to their common destination. The first such trip was one for the scrapbook. Pat rolled up in what could best be described as either a used SUV or four-wheel death chamber, depending on your vantage point. During the weekend in Louisiana, Jens had only spent a short time with Pat, yet had already established a great deal of respect for him. He was eager to begin a new friendship. As Pat approached, Jens instantaneously became aware that MMA was no guarantee for wealth. He inserted himself into the rusty, dilapidated FJ40 Land Cruiser and acknowledged his driver with a reverent "Thank you, Mr. Miletich." Jens would later tell me that addressing Pat as Mr. Miletich lasted about seventy-two days and then morphed into sh-t bag or rat bastard, deference and respect notwithstanding.

At any rate, a combination of awkwardness and safety infractions marred the expedition. Jens noticed that each time Pat turned the vehicle, the seat in which he occupied traveled several inches in the opposite direction of the turn. When the vehicle leveled out and headed straight, again the roving chair would find center ground. If the change of direction was slightly aggressive, so was the abruptness of the seat slide, so much that a "hands out to the side—brace yourself" tactic was required. Jens finally gathered the courage to declare, "Is there something I need to do here with this seat? If you haven't noticed, every time you turn the steering wheel, I am sliding back and forth uncontrollably."

Pat looked over, silently deeming the situation as unimportant, and proclaimed, "Yeah, that seat isn't bolted down; you may want to buckle up."

Jens understood their friendship was in its infancy, and he was comfortable with the Socrates-Plato hierarchy, so he wisely chose to buckle up.

To this day, he still questions how strapping in that night added to his personal safety. If he manages to get around to it, one of his future goals is to question Pat's logic on that maiden voyage. Not that it would change a whole lot; rather, he would like to go on the record for what he feels was an obvious miscalculation. On the rare occasion they would have been in an accident, things wouldn't have gone well—at least not for Jens. Not only would he have been discharged into the windshield like a torpedo, but he would have enjoyed the added benefit of having been strapped in as if he were wearing a straight jacket. However, on this day, seven years earlier, politeness would be the rule of law; and he wasn't about to question the honorable Mr. Miletich.

One of the reasons that Pat and Jens became fast friends is that Jens recognized Pat's emphasis on being a team. The concept of 'team' in the Miletich camp redefines the word. You can use whatever expression you would like to describe these guys.

Call them warriors, competitors, pugilists, brothers, athletes, or whatever you will. If just for a moment you could witness the affection they have for each other, it leaves you speechless. Jens will remind you that this didn't happen automatically, and it isn't for sale. They speak an esoteric language and have a bond that cannot be fabricated, genuinely loving each other. This type of love sets an example for the rest of us. It is not forced or contrived; it's real—a bare bones, no masks, you can't do anything that would make me stop loving you sort of love.

For years, these guys have gone to war together, uncountable hours of grappling, sparring, wrestling, boxing, sweating, hurting, winning, and losing. They have seen the best and the worst of each other, shared the greatest victories, and endured the most devastating losses. When one of these guys loses a fight, they have compared it to experiencing a death. The feeling of loss is so great it can paralyze their very being and eviscerate their identity. At a time like this, the chips are counted. You take a friendship inventory and see who's still standing. Win, lose, or draw, these friendships are unchangeable.

Pat Miletich also has influence. As I mentioned early, Keith leads our Wednesday discussions. However, there is a certain deference paid to Pat. For a guy who admits being hit in the head far too many times, he is stunningly intelligent. His weekly offering of wisdom and discernment is more than you can define in words. I have often been left speechless after Pat shared a prior experience, a story of forgiveness, a mistake he made, a lesson he learned. He would explain how, after a long history of challenges, roadblocks, setbacks, or personal tragedies, his faith has grown and he is blessed beyond his wildest imagination.

Pat has transformed the lives of hundreds of young men and somehow managed to harness and direct their previously misguided rage. He has renovated this energy into positive and constructive output and changed the future of countless men at a tenuous crossroads in their existence.

If a family member, friend, pastor, or preacher were to offer the same exact words to these guys, they may go unheeded. The difference lies in his bona fide credibility. Pat has an undeniable credibility with these blokes, which almost no one else could garner. Each of them realizes and understands that, if Pat asks them to do something, he's done it himself. He can relate to their pain. He can also relate to their dreams and aspirations. They listen to Pat. They confer with Pat. Without hesitation, if he asked, they would go to war for him.

Jens and these men are friends. They are a tribe. They are brothers. They are family. There are times when they will fight, scream, yell, argue, and disagree. Yet their blood, shed many times for each other, will not be shed in vain.

Pat and Jens

(Pat had been politely asked to face the camera,
but none of us had the ability to enforce the request.)

Journey to a
World Champion

I find it difficult to define excellence. The term is often used carelessly and is frequently diluted. To be truly great, I believe, is something few people will ever accomplish. By its definition alone, being truly great must be significantly rare.

Like most everything else in Jens's life, rising to become a world champion would be accomplished through overcoming obstacles. After defeating several worthy opponents, Jens began to climb the fight ladder. His next two bouts would be credible competitors: Alfonso Alcarez and Dave Velasquez. These guys were the real deal, and victories over them would be praiseworthy. Jens steered through these two human roadblocks, and a title shot was in his future.

Jens knew his forthcoming opponent was a machine. This man had quickly dispatched many great fighters with relative ease. His skills were sharp, his mind was tough, and his punches were devastating. If Jens was to get a chance at a title, he first would need to go through a determined fighter named John Lewis.

"He was muscular and tall, and walked around much larger than 155 pounds. I watched him destroy my grappling coach in less than a minute." Jens observed, "He had been around awhile and was well respected. As always, no one gave me a chance."

At the same time as his most important contest, Jens indicated he was nearly crippled. His sciatic nerve was causing him severe pain; he could barely walk. Like a wounded dog, he would limp around until he couldn't take it anymore. If his next destination required crawling sideways to get there, Jens used that method as well. However, there was no way he wouldn't take the match. Jens recalled, "I was broke, needed the money, and these shots don't come around often. Crippled or not, my ass would be in that octagon."

Since their man couldn't stop hobbling, the team of Miletich, Hughes, and Horn devised a plan to hide Jens for the seven days before the fight. They would keep him away from any cameras, interviews, or potential spies, who might reveal this injury. If Lewis knew of his ailment, he would change his game plan accordingly and seek to expose this chink in the Pulver armor.

Instead of fancy training facilities and press conferences, they would transform the hotel room into a rudimentary training ring. "It was ridiculous," Jens recounted. "We took the two beds and stood 'em sideways against each of the far walls. Mattresses were placed on end and any furniture cleared out of the center area. I had a twelve-foot square, and we used this space all week.

"Jeremy Horn gave me the best advice: train easy and rest. He told me it would be better to lie on my butt, and rest, than aggravate the injury with hardcore sparring. I just trusted my team. You can win or lose merely on the advice and game plan of your team."

Now it was time to formulate the fight strategy. Jens had confidence in his team. He felt that, despite the critics' opinions, he would be victorious. Jens explains: "I had the strongest competitor on the planet in Matt Hughes, the most well-rounded athlete in Jeremy Horn, the wizard Pat Miletich in my corner, and the scout master that brought everything together in Monte Cox."

Considering their man's ailing back, the team decided Jens had about one minute to win the fight. Lewis had an impressive ground game and was terribly strong; it would be bad news for Jens if the battle went to the mat. They watched tapes and studied the style of their opponent. Almost immediately, they saw that a favorite tactic of Lewis was to flick a jab. Usually effective, this enabled him to control the agenda.

The Miletich team took the unorthodox approach of having Jens eat a few of those jabs, if necessary. They figured Lewis would jab, move side to side, and jab again. If Jens had to take a few of these on the chin or forehead, that would be the price to pay for the upcoming strategy. Jens was going to trade getting hit with a bevy of stinging jabs for the singular opportunity to throw his overhand left. The calculation was for Jens to throw it with all his power, might, and force; if it landed, it would be lights out.

Sure enough, just as if a screenplay came to life, *wham,* Jens landed the punch directly on the jawline of Lewis. Perhaps no human could have remained standing. "He was like Bambi on ice," Jens explained.

Lewis crumpled to the ground, out cold; instantaneously, Jens Pulver had done it again. He proved everyone wrong. Experts and enthusiasts had discarded him as the next stepping stone for Lewis, the "real" contender. No one gave him a chance. No one bet on him. No one believed in his abilities. No one, that is, except Jens and his teammates.

Before the bout, Jens had a conversation with Big John McCarthy, the referee of the match and a much-liked personality of the UFC. He asked John if he could have his black-and-white referee jersey after the contest. Jens explained, "He said he doesn't give away his shirts, so I pressed on."

"Big John, what's it going to take? I really want that shirt as a souvenir of my big night." Jens told me that John said if he knocked him out in the first round, the shirt was his.

In retrospect, he believes that, in John's mind, he had made a safe bet. He could have said "If you ride into the octagon on a unicorn, wear a bikini and tap shoes into the ring, and hypnotize Lewis with some Tinker Bell fairy dust, you can have the shirt." In reality, most people didn't think Jens had a chance to win.

After that ruinous left hand landed and Lewis collapsed to the mat, Jens took care of a few items of business. He delivered two messages. He acknowledged his corner of Miletich, Hughes, and Horn with a perfectly laid plan. Then he quickly made eye contact with Big John McCarthy, Jens signaling to John and pointing at his chest, saying, in effect, "*My* shirt, brother; that's *my* shirt."

Later that night, John set out to locate Jens and delivered on his word. Jens recounted, "Big John kept his promise, and I have always admired him for that. The old-school style shirt is hanging in my closet even today."

Another memorable night was in the books. Like most things a professional athlete faces, the focus for the next goal quickly takes center stage. The celebration would be brief, and all energies would be directed toward the battle that lay ahead.

This battle, however, had unprecedented consequences for Jens. It would be a title shot. The years of sweat, blood, tears, and suffering would be put to the test. The chance of a lifetime was on the horizon. Jens knew, in the depths of his soul, that he had to perform. One more time, he would need to prove the critics wrong. And although he had plenty of practice at this task, each time he also had to face the demon of self-doubt. When you have been told all your life that you will fail, the voices of uncertainty often get your attention. They attempt to convince you of their legitimacy and authority. These voices attempt to define you.

Uno, Dos, Bacon Night

Many people were in attendance during the bout with John Lewis, yet few were more important than a man named Dana White. He was in the front row and witnessed Jens's crushing left blow that ended the match. Even though this punch left an impression on the jaw of Lewis, it turns out that it left more of an impression on the psyche of Mr. White, future president of the UFC.

A short while later, brothers Frank and Lorenzo Fertitta (Zuffa, Inc.) purchased the UFC. Dana was charged with the task of creating the absolute best matches possible. In the 155-pound weight class, Jens Pulver had emerged. Yet, in everyone's mind, the undisputed best fighter was a warrior in Japan called Caol Uno. His talents were considered far above any competitor, and he had just recently conquered Rumina Sato, widely thought to be the second most credible combatant.

Before Jens dispatched Lewis, most predicted the title fight would consist of Lewis and Uno. However, Jens had other plans. Dana understood that the match that everyone was talking about was Caol Uno versus Jens Pulver.

The venue would be Atlantic City, New Jersey, at the Taj Mahal Casino and Resort. This would be the biggest stage Jens had ever seen. His nerves danced each time he envisioned the upcoming melee. He knew the doubters would begin to chirp, and they did. If you listened to any of the prefight commentary, the tale was the same: Caol would own Jens Pulver. He would sprawl and brawl, get Jens on the ground, and destroy him. Insiders didn't believe Jens was in his league—not remotely.

The critics prophesied that this would be a quick night; Uno would barely break a sweat. Knowing full well what the experts were forecasting, Jens became aware he had nothing to lose and simply returned to basics, to the formula that had allowed him to travel this far. He went back to his team.

The brain trust of Miletich, Hughes, and Horn would be tested again. Jens recounted, "We were nightmares. We were hungry like animals and trained all day. I loved my guys, and I counted on them for everything. On the upside of my life, you would not want to challenge me. You didn't have a prayer. On the downside, when self-doubt would creep in, it wasn't the same. I would spend my existence in a shallow temple, battling the mad voices in my head."

Currently, at this point in his life, everything was clicking. His training, physical conditioning, and technical skills were blade sharp. Whether or not Uno, the press, and UFC insiders were aware of it, Jens Pulver was about to bring the house down.

Two days before the trek to New Jersey, Jens walked into Pat's office and noticed something on the table. It was Pat's world championship belt. Although it wasn't resting in a glass display case accompanied by red laser security beams, to Jens this was the most precious jewel of its kind: priceless. The currency that it took to own this symbol of achievement wasn't traded on the open market. Whether you were rich, powerful or connected, there was only a single way to a world title: you had to earn it. No matter where you lived or what country you called home, you had to be better than anyone else in the world. As Jens exited Pat's office, his inner voice spoke to him with a quiet confidence. Jens knew in his heart he was going to win this match and become a champion.

Physically, Jens was in extremely good shape. After seeking treatment for his ailing back, with a local chiropractor, he was moving freely and with limited pain. It was critical that Jens did not have any handicaps while facing the likes of Caol Uno. Jens knew he didn't want to be on the ground with this man. He and Jeremy had trained ceaselessly, preparing a proper sprawl and takedown defense. If Jens could keep the bout on its feet, his chances for victory would be multiplied.

Just before the match, Jens sat patiently in the locker room and reviewed his game plan over and over in his head. By now his hands were taped, his muscles warm, and his thoughts in the right place. He explained, "I just pushed everything out of my mind and concentrated on what I needed to do. I didn't want to lose. I needed to keep on winning each bout. As the entry music plays and you walk down the aisle, there is no turning back."

After the brief introductions from the ring announcer, Big John McCarthy uttered those famous commencing words: "Let's get it on."

Within minutes of the first round, Uno managed to "get his back." In MMA vernacular, this is equivalent to maximum bad news. When your opponent has your back, there are many options for him to potentially end the bout. You are susceptible to a rear naked choke (requiring submission); strikes that cannot be adequately defended; or, equally disastrous, your rival can control you.

Jens disclosed to me, "I was scared to be on the ground with him. As soon as he got my back, I thought, sh-t, this is going to be over before I know it. I had to stay calm. I just said to myself, stay calm, or this is over."

After managing to disengage from Uno's powerful hold, Jens took the match where it needed to be for him—on his feet. It was here that Jens could begin to impose his will and regulate the bout. Each time Uno would shoot for his legs, Jens used his takedown defense and wrestling skills to counter the effort. As he returned to his corner after the first round, he realized that, if he listened to Pat and employed the team's predetermined strategy, things would come together.

Subsequent rounds were nothing short of all-out wars. As confident as you are in the plan, getting hit in the face has a way of distracting you from meeting the agenda. Although you have calculated the plan for success, the other guy in the ring has absolutely no incentive for you to implement it. He, like you, is after the same Holy Grail. The only problem is there's only one of these up for grabs.

Steadily, Jens began to impose his will. He described the events: "I chased him everywhere. I wasn't letting him take me down. I was able to establish ring generalship."

When a fighter is able to control and direct the contest, many times the foe becomes utterly frustrated and begins to make mistakes. Jens was unrelenting. He explained, "I was not going to walk backwards. Under no circumstances was I going to allow him to dictate the fight. If I got knocked out, so be it, I'd get knocked out chasing him around the ring. For twenty-five minutes, I pressed the action. If I was moving forward, that meant he could not. I took his game plan and implemented it myself."

As the final seconds ticked off the clock, the decision was in the judges' hands.

Jens and Caol had completed an epic duel. The fans had received more than they could have imagined. Two great athletes gave every ounce they had. Both fighters left everything in the ring, their efforts archived as a clash for the ages. They had great respect and admiration for each other as they waited for the ruling. Although there were no losers this night, only one man could hold the title. Only one man would be crowned world champion.

Jens, unsure of who would be declared the winner, asked Pat and Jeremy who they thought won the contest. Pat, scarcely able to control himself, declared, "Jens, you won the fight. I am sure of it; you won this fight."

Even though he recognized that Pat and his team did not have final authority on the decision, he also trusted their opinion. Pat, Matt, and Jeremy were all confident that Jens was victorious. As Jens and Caol met in the middle of the ring to hear the verdict, his heart raced, and his skin was prickly with anticipation. As the scoring was read out loud, Big John McCarthy slowly raised Jens Pulver's hand. He had won the title. Instantly, tears began to rain down.

Jens explained to me: "These were tears for my team, tears for all that training. I saw my brother Able and his girlfriend Trish in the crowd. I just put my head in my hands and cried."

Jens had accomplished the impossible. He had beaten the odds. After a lifetime of abuse, struggles, and heartache, he had climbed the mountain. He not only conquered a fierce competitor in Caol Uno, but he had also destroyed his father's predictions, which were so pessimistic, they were lathered in failure, misery, and hopelessness. Tonight, however, there was pure joy. As the squad of Miletich, Hughes, and Horn jumped up and down like little kids, Jens quickly made it back to his corner to celebrate.

A dream had been accomplished, yet it wasn't without costs. Thousands of hours of sweat equity had been invested. There were uncountable memories of what this endeavor consumed.

At times, his muscles were so sore, he could barely get out of bed. The endless days of grappling, boxing, wrestling, lifting, running, and sparring would send most guys packing. Not Jens. The payoff was too great. He upheld that most everything in life of true value is achieved through hard work and suffering. This extraordinary triumph was no different, and now his achievement was memorialized. Just two days earlier, he had gazed at Pat's world title belt, and now he had his own. As it was wrapped around his waist, he took a deep breath, collected his thoughts, and reflected on all of the coaches, teammates and friends who had helped on the journey. It was a collective effort and was priceless. Jens Pulver was a world champion.

Pat Miletich once advised the Wednesday group that, when you become a champion and possess the belt, there's only one problem: you now have to defend it. Jens was able to successfully defend the title in his next two clashes. He defeated Dennis Hallman in a five-round war and, months later, was pitted against "the Prodigy," B. J. Penn. Although it sounds like a broken record, Jens heard all of the same rumblings as his match with Penn approached. The insiders, once again, predicted that Penn was more skillful, talented, and tenacious. And although (years later) B. J. Penn would attain the goal of owning a title belt, it wouldn't be through a win over Jens Pulver. To the surprise of all Jens's critics, the duel lasted the entire five rounds and inevitably went to the judges' scorecards. Once again, his hand was raised. Jens had defeated B. J. and the thousands of expert opinions. Time and time again, Jens proved everyone wrong.

In life, we are constantly reminded that success can be momentary, and guarantees are fool's gold. The next stage of life for Jens was proof of this. An unexpected UFC contract dispute arose, and when the dust settled, he found himself vacating his title as lightweight champion. He would begin the next chapter of his career battling in smaller, lesser-known venues. Jens would end up winning his next two fights, then unexpectedly losing his two subsequent battles. Attempting to get back to his winning ways, his next venue was back in the Quad Cities, and the weigh-in was at a neighboring bar.

The night was sponsored by the local pork producers. As unique and bizarre as it sounds, you could have all the free bacon you could eat; in addition, there was a bonus. For the low, low price of one dollar, you could add lettuce, tomato, and bread. That's right, for a buck you could devour a big, fat BLT. During one of our Wednesday meetings, Jens illustrated how fleeting fame and success can be. He explained, "It was over that quick; the phone stops ringing, and the money stops flowing, just like that [snap]. One day, I was world champion, proceeded to successfully defend my title, then *bam, bam,* got knocked out twice, and I was at bacon night."

As Jens learned with his career, momentum can indeed be transitory. And unless you fully commit to your endeavor, it, too, can fade away. Although the Wednesday group was presently clicking on all cylinders and lives were changing, there was an empty chair again. It was the chair that had previously belonged to Jens.

Jens becomes world champion at the Taj Mahal Casino and
Resort in Atlantic City, New Jersey.

AWOL

Jens had been AWOL for many, many weeks, and some of us had heard disconcerting reports. We had been briefed that Jens was holed up in his room, spending eighteen to twenty hours a day on the computer, instead of advancing his physical or emotional state. He would later reveal that plugging away on video games was the only place he felt safe. It was here that he didn't have to relate to the reality of his world. He was, in a sense, in a coma. It was easier to battle demons in cyberspace than those fighting for space in his mind.

On a Wednesday morning, as I walked into Pat's gym, to my surprise, I saw Jens in my peripheral vision. He was sitting alone in the square footage of the gym that housed PowerBars, sports drinks, training equipment and T-shirts. The apparel options were of a coherent theme. You could adorn yourself in shirts from the Matt Hughes Collection, Tim "the Maine-iac" Sylvia's assortment, the Pat Miletich MFS Elite group, or my personal favorite, a plain black shirt with white lettering, reminding humankind that "Your Kung Fu Is No Good Here."

As I approached, he didn't even look up, perhaps because he was engrossed in his IPOD selections but more likely because he didn't want to be bothered. He admits that it's a short trip between the two words "Jens" and "grumpy." As I leaned on the table waiting for him to acknowledge me, a minute or two passed. There was a nonaggressive competition between us, as to who was going to give up first. I thought about capitulating. I had been warned that you don't press Jens. If he thinks he is being forced, pushed, or lectured, then you're about to have a bad day. He will promptly let you know that you better get out of his face or the dogs may start barking. And if the dogs start barking, you need to hope the tensile strength of the leash will hold.

He finally glanced up, earphones still in place. I signaled a request that he remove the earphones and tenderly asked if he would be joining us upstairs.

"Nah," he responded, in a dismissive manner. "I'm tired and I'm going to be getting something to eat here, right quick."

I carefully remembered the edict not to press Jens and simply responded, "We would really love you back in the group, Jens."

He issued a half nod, and I knew my airtime had expired.

Kevin walked by. I caught up with him in the passageway. Knowing that, if I let him know I had just asked Jens the same question, he would be less than compelled, I omitted that part but encouraged Kevin to approach him. "Go ask Jens if he's interested in the discussion today; he might listen to you," I assured.

If Jens got pissed at him and got out of his chair, Kevin's wrestling background offered a better takedown defense than I could offer. I might have a slight advantage over Kevin if it came to a standup encounter, but Jens's spiteful left hook would penetrate either guard, so I deemed that irrelevant. Although I did not have the authority to make such a decision, I figured that, if Kevin got decked, it was worth the risk.

As I patiently sat upstairs in my gray, cushy chair, I waited for the result of Kevin's inquiry. Feeling half guilty for knowingly throwing my buddy under the bus, I sensed that, if necessary, I would ask for and likely receive his forgiveness.

Just then, my surrogate older brother approached me; he shook his head, sat down slightly irritated, and scolded me with "you jackass." I responded the only way I could think of; I tattled on him. Keith was a couple seats away and, with a spirit of shamelessness, I evoked, "Keith, we have gathered here today as brothers in fellowship, and Kevin insists on calling me names. I was sitting here, minding my own business, and his potty mouth ignited. Please make him stop."

Keith appeared to be confused and said, "What are you idiots talking about?" I then rose to the level of statesmanlike diplomat and asked that we let bygones be bygones. Kevin got one last "jackass" in for the record, and we moved forward accordingly. He notified me that Jens was not making the session and, by now, he was fully annoyed.

As I contemplated the thought of Jens never returning, there was a nauseating feeling inside my stomach. I knew we gave it our level best effort; however, I had come to the conclusion that Jens would not be back. In fact, we were convinced of it. Convinced, that is, until an old face showed up at Pat's gym.

He had the face of pure determination. He had the face of a guy who wasn't in the mood to give up. He had the face of a guy who had a singular goal that day. The first question he asked me: "Where's Jens?"

Big Rit

I have called him a friend for twenty years; his name is Todd Rittenhouse. Standing six feet three, weighing two hundred pounds, with a sculpted physique, he was Big Rit to us, someone I want to be like when I grow up. It is nearly impossible to believe that one guy could consistently demonstrate qualities of kindness, generosity, wisdom, love, strength, forgiveness, and intelligence. Yet Todd has them all. I met him in my sophomore year of high school, and we spent a few years together on the same ball diamond. He was a stud athlete, and I was fortunate to have him as a teammate.

Todd teaches history at a high school not far from the Quad Cities. With his endless list of abilities, he is a blessing to scores of kids. He will undoubtedly be the teacher his students tell their children about. While some of us provide lip service to certain challenges, Todd reviews the landscape, determines a plan, and gets it done. He married his high school sweetheart and is in the process of raising four beautiful children. Many years back, he made a pledge to his wife that she could stay at home and be with the kids; he felt they would be better served. However, to accomplish this, there would be sacrifices. For the last seven years, Todd has worked two jobs, many weeks totaling seventy hours or more. Three nights a week, he works from 11:00 PM to 7:00 AM. Even more impressively, he never complains. He remains an inspiration to me.

Todd and Jens had met several years before. Like so many people who were introduced to Todd, Jens was awestruck. Jens told me that he always held a deep respect for him. He watched the way Todd interacted with his children and wife, and he said he couldn't understand how a guy that big was so kind and gentle. Jens once mentioned to me, "He's such an amazing father. I use him as my example of how I should act and behave."

They had not seen each other for a long time, and Jens had no idea that we had recruited Todd. This would be a reunion and an unexpected one.

The reason Big Rit attended the study was because he had been invited by a guy named Gary. Backing up several months, I encouraged Gary to consider showing up to our weekly meeting. I went to high school with him, as well. Until recently, I hadn't seen him much over the past fifteen years. The previous fall, he attended a small group that met at our house on Sunday nights.

Although we could go deep, shirt-off-your-back mode if necessary, our primary relationship was fashioned upon the ability to harass each other. In terms of verbal jabs, whenever we engaged, there was sort of a virtual, hidden scoreboard that would tally who could outwit the other. Although Gary was conversant on many subjects, our exchanges were plagued and enshrined with the unfortunate propensity for him to malaprop. A famous boxer once said, "I may just fade off into Bolivian."

As painful as that quote may be to one's ears, Gary's misuse of the English language would actually result in your head throbbing. Many of our debates would be headed to the judges for a decision ruling when, in the last round, Gary would use a word like "caveat" where it didn't belong. There would be an odd and seemingly endless pause, both of us knowing he wished he could rewind the clock and take the word back. However, the contest was over: a self-administered TKO.

Despite the repeated penchant for using nonapplicable words at just the wrong time, Gary's talent is evangelism. Not in the sense of some hokey, phony, late-night infomercial, but rather in the genuine "get your ass to this group" sense. He handed out more summonses to appear than any one of us, and his success rate was impressive. Today, Big Rit was in the house, and it was all because of Gary.

After Jens had declined my invite and Kevin's invite, we knew that we had one last chance. We sent Todd to find him, sat back, and said a quick, yet deliberate prayer. It took about two seconds, and the direction of Jens's life would forever change. He saw Big Rit and immediately was on a dead run. He leaped up and embraced Todd's massive frame, squeezed and hugged him to an extent that can't properly be described. The force of the clinch would compress the vital organs of most other beings. Although most people do not get to tell Jens what to do, Todd bluntly informed him, "You're coming with me."

Kevin and I looked at each other. Without exchanging words, we knew our brother was back in our group. Jens Pulver was back, and this time it was for good. In terms of answering prayers, I've been told that God is never in a hurry, but his timing is always perfect.

Although we did not ask for an explanation, Jens apologized for his absence. He equated it to taking an antibiotic. He said that although the instructions and doctor inform you to take the medicine until the bottle is entirely empty, many people will stop ingesting the medicine when they begin to feel better. Jens had been to our group many times and had begun to feel healthier, refreshed, restored, and recovered. He assumed these feelings would continue. They didn't.

Jens described the last several weeks: "I had fires and flames inside. It's all emotions right now, and I'm losing the battle. The reason I am back in this group is because it's not about money, prestige, or who you are. The thing I love about you guys is that you're here to help. It's about the experience, loyalty, and trust. This group is here for me or anyone who needs it. It's not how you got here; it's simply that you're here. People have no idea how rare this is. How difficult it is to have someone actually listen to your story. I never thought I was good enough for church. This is my church."

If you trace back what had taken place, to have Jens back in the group, it's hard to believe. The people, prayers, and circumstances that were woven together for this to occur were chilling. Some call it a coincidence, but not these guys. It is mind boggling to me how God's plan is revealed. I truly believe that our Creator had been enthusiastically pursuing Jens. God wanted him on the team. He knew how special he is. He knew how many lives Jens would affect. As humans, we often try to control everything, as if we are in charge. We falsely believe that our hands need to be on the steering wheel. When, in fact, all we need to do is let go and let God.

Big Rit and Jens

To date, over one hundred and twenty men have attended
the Wednesday group at Pat's gym.

Peanut Butter

With Jens back in the group, I understood the sessions could be many things; yet of all the infinite possibilities, boring was not one of them. Loyalty can be an overused and underappreciated word, but not on Wednesdays. We cover a vast array of topics from Jesus to peanut butter, and today it was the latter. After an opening prayer, occasionally Keith would ask if anyone in the group was currently struggling with something. If so, we would attempt to use the hour for helping the person, guiding him, exchanging experiences, offering advice, or sometimes just listening.

When Keith asked his question today, Big Ben jumped in. Ben stands a mere six feet five and weighs in at 265 pounds: an ominous figure with paws the size of a grizzly. In quick order, you learn that one of his most appealing qualities is that raw truth exits his mouth. It may not be everyone's truth; but undoubtedly, it's Ben's.

There were times directly following a deep, thought-provoking, symbolic passage from scripture, with many attendees in full absorption mode, when Ben would launch a verbal MOAB (Mother of All Bombs). "I don't care what any-one says. No one walked on water; that's bullsh-t. He might have been a great man, a great teacher, done great things, but nobody walked on water."

Notwithstanding the inadvertent, borderline blasphemy, Keith had repeatedly calibrated every one of us to understand that this was a safe environment for any comment, any question or any debate.

Ben was struggling that day with how to deal with a friend and roommate who, despite continued requests to cease such action, had been ridiculing him on a daily basis. The Fox Sports Network had been at Pat's gym for a couple of days, covering the fighters and their daily rituals. Ben indicated this friend was telling everyone (including the TV news crew) that he was crazy, bizarre, and compulsive. His roommate goes on to explain that, in an attempt to fend off any peanut butter bandits, Ben takes pictures of his current jars and related inventory. Truth be told, Ben did take Polaroids of his favorite creamy bread spread. However, in his mind, this was a preemptive and necessary undertaking to catch a repeat offender in the unsavory act of thievery.

Ben explained his love affair with peanut butter and, although he enjoyed it immensely, explained he was willing to share under certain circumstances. Parting with this allocation of sacred supply meant that you needed to be truthful if Ben ever inquired, "How much did you eat?" If he felt you were lacking veracity with your answer, there would be hell to pay. Today, hell would be paid in full.

Ben looked at Pat and said, "I'm getting pissed off, and I want it to stop."

Pat, who was navigating between problem solving and a belly laugh, quietly said, "Ben, you gotta admit, that's pretty funny." That was not the answer Ben was looking for. There was a pause. Pat continued: "Ben, I don't think he's trying to hurt your feelings; he knows he was getting your goat, so he kept it up. I'll handle it."

"Now, *I'm pissed*," roared Jens from the outer circle, at a decibel level not often heard on Wednesdays. He continued: "Pat, you better fix this and fix it fast or I'm going to f---ing knock someone out. You hear me? If he makes fun of Ben for this, one more time, I'll shatter his jaw. Ben told him to stop, told him again, and told him again. Enough is enough."

A few of the newest members of the group were struck by the queer juxtaposition of Jesus's spirit in the room and the F-bomb dropping. Yet, most of us just bathed in the calm anticipation of Pat's upcoming reply. As with most things he handled, it was masterful. He simply replied, "Jensy, I told you I would take care of it, and please *quit cursing*. You know you are not to curse in the gym. I will handle it, Jens. I promise you; I will handle it."

Jens replied, "OK, but you know I ain't playin'. The man told him to stop."

Never

After a few minutes of guys exchanging nonverbal, holy balls what just happened, and eye-reading communication, we broke off into small groups. As odds would have it, Jens, Pat, and I were in the same unit. I was sitting on the wrestling mat with my back against the wall. Jens was standing next to me, still a bit fidgety from the earlier exchange. I made the determination that his heart rate had gone from anaerobic to normal levels, leaned over, and said, "Jens, that was a unique illustration; yet I admire your fierce loyalty to Ben."

He turned my way, looked down, and, in a serious, menacing tone, advised me of the following: "If you're my friend, if you're on my team, no one better mess with your peanut butter."

Don't make me use these.

The Injustice Police

To become a friend of Jens is not a terribly easy task, and it has nothing to do with his degree of likeability. Rather, he doesn't allow many people to enter his world. However, if you manage to traverse the minefield and become a companion, you abruptly learn one important fact: Jens hates injustice. Perhaps the word "hate" might not even be adequate to capture his sentiment. It might be too delicate. Words like detest, abhor, revolt, and loathe better encapsulate his feeling on the subject. In terms of who decides what the definition for injustice might be, don't look for a jury of twelve. There is no courtroom, judge, or jury to be found. This unseen police force doesn't ride around in squad cars, don badges, or carry weapons. In fact, the organizational chart has only one name: Jens Pulver. If, by chance, you have made the ill-fated decision to impose your bullying, rage, or maltreatment onto a smaller, younger recipient, I suggest you drop to your knees and pray. It's a simple prayer. It might sound something like this: "Lord, I realize there are eight billion of your creations walking the earth right now; but please verify that Jens Pulver is not within a sixty-mile radius of me. Amen."

The fact that Jens nearly got his brains beaten out of his head during his childhood is enough to set the course on the topic. Even if it's for a split second, if he thinks a larger, stronger individual is about to attempt some bullying tactics, things are about to go South.

"I'll bully the bully," declared Jens, in a conversation we had. He has informed me on many occasions that he must carefully choose where to spend his time. Public gatherings, large crowds, bars, or similar establishments are often excluded from the list. For whatever reason, in today's society, when large numbers of people gather, someone frequently finds it necessary to establish himself as the self-defined Alpha male. This grade school mentality is predictably amplified when alcohol is inserted into the mix. If Jens believes the perceived bullying is being delivered to a woman or child, magnify the bring-your-house-down meter by a factor of ten. Yet, even if a smaller guy is getting picked on or made fun of, his skin starts to crawl.

His heart begins to swell and previously dormant emotions begin to permeate through his system. He thinks about what it would have been like, so many years ago, if someone had come to his aid. He thinks about how grateful he would have been if a stranger had pulled his bullying father off his mother before he beat her senseless. How he would have felt if someone had grabbed his dad by his shirt collar and said, "If you ever knock your son off his bicycle again, I'm going to end your days on this planet."

He also wonders whether intervention is the best option or if it's going to inflame the aggressor to a new level. As the hurried barrage of thoughts races through his mind, he is confident of only one thing: there won't be any bullies on his watch.

During one of our Wednesday sessions, Jens was extremely curious about what God would allow or find acceptable, as it related to his enforcement of *perceived* justice. On this particular day, the discussion centered on forgiveness or how we are to deal with difficult situations and people. Many of us are trying to better understand how to cope with conflict or unresolved baggage in our lives. As I took several deep breaths and tried to clear my head, I thought to myself that I had better listen carefully. On my long inventory list of personal developmental needs, forgiveness issues were at the top. If I believe someone has wronged me, I have a difficult time with forgiving and forgetting. And, unfortunately, have come to the delusional conclusion that hitting them in the face may be the answer to smooth out any issues. As I surveyed the room, I noticed my friends had closely focused their eyes on Keith. This topic had resonated with me, Jens, and the group. With undivided attention, we waited for Mr. Nester to begin today's class.

Although there were twenty-five guys in the room, it just so happened that Jens was in the chair directly to my right. As if you were in a movie theater or business meeting, there is an unwritten rule we collectively needed to follow. Shortly before our session commenced, it was standard operating procedure for us to ensure our cell phones were in the off position. At the very least, we had to select the manner mode option; but even incessant vibrating was quite distracting. A few minutes into our discussion, I observed Jens answering his phone. Had I been leading a business meeting, I would have given stink eye to the perpetrator, without saying a word. This circumstance was quite different. Without attempting to listen to his conversation, I was eighteen inches from him and overheard him whisper into the phone, "Mom, I'm in church right now. I have to call you back. OK, I love you, bye."

I just sat there and smiled to myself. Although I was determined, a minute earlier, to absorb every spoken word, I became distracted, and my thoughts began to spin. I thought back to the first day I saw Jens in Las Vegas and pondered how we could gently convince him to attend our group. I remembered the innumerable invites we had given him and his refusal to accept. Pat had told Kevin that, come hell or high water, he was going to get Jens in this group, and I reflected on the first day Jens sat with us. Feelings, emotions, pain, and struggles poured from his heart.

Before we knew it, Jens had come and gone, many of us convinced he would not be back. We thought he might bury himself in his thoughts of darkness, fear, and doubt. We wanted Jens to see the way, the truth, and the life. We hoped and prayed he would come back to his brothers. Today, he was not only back, but he was letting his mom know he would promptly return her call. Jens would call her back after *church* was over.

Within a few minutes, I was able to gather myself and focus my attention on the present dialogue. As we discussed the scripture that speaks about turning the other cheek, and that vengeance is not for us, Jens, with a challenging tone, piped in: "Hold on a second. I have a question. I understand that we're not to just go out and beat someone up; that part is clear. What I want to know is … can we come to someone's aid or rescue?"

Keith half smiled as he fielded the inquiry. He was prepared for follow-up to probe deeper into Jens's question; however, he also knew he would be going for a ride. As he noticed Jens leaning forward on the edge of his chair, with a determined, curious look, he knew what was ahead. In fact, we all knew. Keith, in a calm, calculated move, tried to frame the hypothetical with a little more specificity. "Jens, give me an example; what exactly do you mean?" Keith planted his feet on the ground, grabbed the virtual straps and carabiners attached to his chair, and clipped in. It appeared Jens had about twenty examples and wanted to contemporaneously unleash the hounds.

"All right, let's say I'm on the playground and some guy, three times the size of another kid, is giving him a beating. The smaller kid is on the ground, helpless, and getting half his ass torn off. Am I supposed to turn the other cheek? Hell, no, I'm not. I'm going over there. I'm going to say, 'You want someone smaller to beat on, you got 'im right here, boy.'"

Keith attempts to jump in: "Jens, hold on … Jens."

"No, I'm not quite done yet. You know that turn-the-other-cheek stuff only goes so far with me. I'm going to bully the bully. If I don't, the bully is going to get away with his sh-t."

By now, a couple things were apparent. Jens was fired up; Keith had his hands full; and everyone was interested in the discussion. One of the reasons this group is so amazing and successful is the openness of opinions. There is no judging or correcting. There may be debate or disagreements, but no one ever gets judged. That's why it's safe. That's why it's beautiful. That's why it's real.

Keith was careful not to pour gasoline on the Pulver brush-fire and said, "You first have to ask where your heart is. I don't believe God would be upset with you or anyone for helping someone in need; you just can't take the situation beyond the remedy. If you stop the bully's actions and calm the situation, that's one thing. If you land fifteen left hooks and proceed to choke him out for good measure, now we're on a slippery slope."

Just like a dog scratching at the front door to be let out, Jens could barely wait for the last syllable from Keith. He wanted to rush in with his rebuttal but displayed good manners and decent self-control as he waited his turn. As Keith finished, Jens jumped in with, "Yeah, but what if he really deserved it?"

Although we tried to contain ourselves, about ten guys broke out in laughter. It was like one of those scenes, at church or the dinner table or a meeting, when you held your hand over your mouth and your body shook. You attempted to control your laughter, thought about serious or even dark topics, and tried to change your thought pattern. It was unsuccessful. In less then ten seconds, the remaining fifteen threw in the towel, and all twenty-five attendees, including Jens, laughed out loud. Jens left his chair. "I'm freaking serious! What if someone really deserved it? Would God be mad at us if we knocked someone out because they had it coming?"

I looked around the room to discover my brothers in various states of amusement. Some were wiping laughter tears from their eyes. Others were slouched in their chairs with one arm across the belly and the opposite hand on the face, vibrating in their seats. The balance of guys were simply laughing and rotating to see their other buddies laughing, which, in turn, created an expansion of uproarious cackling. It took another five minutes for the gang to gather our collective composure.

After the hysterics subsided, we addressed questions. The topic was of paramount importance to almost everyone in the room. We were sitting in a congregation of men who, on many occasions, use brute force to solve problems. Unfortunately, that rarely solves anything. Keith recognized this and, without exactly equating it to a ubiquitous bumper sticker—"What Would Jesus Do?"—asked the group to take inventory of their true intentions. He reminded us that Jesus equals love. We are to love our enemies and treat others the way we want to be treated. If we would simply run our behavior through that litmus test, it's a fail-safe program: simple but not easy.

As Jens described the playground scenario to the group, and before all of the uncontrollable laughter, my eyes started to well up with tears. Because I was sitting next to him, I took off my glasses and acted like I had something in my eyes. I did my best to hide the fact that my emotions had overtaken me. I wasn't embarrassed; rather, I just didn't want to interrupt his dialogue. I thought back to a conversation I had with his mom. Although I believe that there were probably many times when the exact circumstances that Jens described at the schoolyard took place, I wondered if it was also a metaphor for several of his childhood memories.

Marlene told me there were times when the boys' father came home drunk out of his mind, fried on drugs. Pissed off, with nothing better to do, he was determined to lay his hands on someone. The crime the boys were to be punished for was usually half-baked or purely invented. After herding the boys into a room for an inexcusable interrogation, he would look to assign blame for some minor infraction.

Her voice broken, unsuccessfully holding back tears, Marlene described to me the way in which Jens would protect his siblings, especially Able: "If Able was responsible for something, albeit minor or unintentional, Jens would stand up and declare, 'I did it; it was me.'"

Barely decipherable, Marlene went on: "Jens would take a terrible whipping, even if he had nothing to do with it. He loved his brother that much. If the option was to take a beating or hear Able scream out in fear and pain, Jens would rather have it done to him. He would suffer so his brother didn't have to."

If Jens senses maltreatment or someone in need, his inner voice begins a conversation, and it becomes a requirement for him to act. It's automatic. The Injustice Police inside Jens are not fully dedicated to stopping aggression; their scope has a much broader agenda. If Jens thinks someone's basic needs are not being met, he responds immediately and always does so under the radar screen. While most of us are primarily concerned with our own necessities, he has turned the pyramid upside down. Once, I was sitting at the dining room table in Monte Cox's home, and we were discussing our mutual friend.

He chimed in: "Probably the biggest secret about Jens is how much he does for other people. He is constantly trying to help underprivileged children. It also doesn't matter how tough things are currently going for him; it never dissuades him. He never wanted to be famous or noticed. He doesn't look for the camera; he helps when no one else is looking."

A few years ago, when Jens visited a homeless shelter, Monte informed me that, shortly after Jens arrived, he became aware that the children did not have pillows to rest their heads on at night. Within a minute, he disappeared, and no one knew his whereabouts. The group he was with suspected he either got freaked out or became despondent at the situation. They believed he got in his car and left the scene. About forty minutes had passed, and Jens was back at the shelter. Monte recalled, "He took off and went to the store. Jens returned with a car full of pillows. He handed these out, one by one, until every child in the shelter had one. For a guy who has the hardest hands in the sport, Jens has the softest heart of anyone I know."

Mentoring, coaching, and even protecting young kids have always been
requirements for Jens.

Band of Brothers

A little over four hundred years ago, in *The Life of King Henry the Fifth*, Shakespeare wrote, "We few, we happy few, we band of brothers." I don't believe he was speaking about casual, run-of-the-mill acquaintances; he was referring to a group of men who, without pause, would do anything for their comrades. After learning a little bit about Pat Miletich, Monte Cox, and Jens's other friends, I began to understand the parallels. This brotherhood is rare, matchless, and distinctive. These are the same men who own sovereign territory in Jens's inner circle. They are his happy few.

Matt Pena is a gifted boxing coach. However, his best coaching often takes place when no one is wearing gloves. His philosophy, gentle voice, and optimistic outlook are most commonly delivered over lunch or in casual conversation. He and Jens have become extremely close friends over the last couple of years. Pena explains: "As far as the coaching goes, Jens is so talented and had such a good boxing base, I just worked on refinements. Whereas some guys take a long time to develop their skills, Jens picks up everything I teach him right away. When I started working with him, he had already been a champion and was currently competing overseas. I was already working with Hughes, Sylvia, and Fisher, so when Jens and I began our partnership, it just seemed like a perfect fit."

Matt informed me that, when he first met Jens, he was struck by his straightforwardness. He thought, "Well, I don't have to read this guy's mind. Some people aren't comfortable with this type of candidness, yet it works well for me. It doesn't take long to find out what kind of person he is; you learn right away that he cares about people. At times, he will come across as antisocial and high-strung. Other times, he reveals his character and you are blown away."

Pena, as his closest friends refer to him, finishes by advising me why he cares so much about his friend: "There are days where Jens will bark, moan, and complain; however, those of us who know him well understand his bark is worse than his bite. Deep down, we know his heart. One day I was having a conversation with him, and he was in one of the Jens moods. He was growling, snarling, and moaning. He was acting all ticked off, acting tough, and then I mentioned that one of my boxing students was upset because he couldn't compete in a national tournament."

Jens inquired, "Why can't he go? What's the deal?"

Matt described to Jens that he didn't have the money to afford the travel and entry fee. Jens, still grumbling from his earlier tantrum, told Matt he would handle it. It took just a short while, and Jens had secured a plane ticket valued at over five hundred dollars. Matt thanked him and even made an offer for the family to repay Jens, but he refused. Jens informed Matt of just one condition that day: "Don't tell anyone where this came from, do you hear me, Pena? Don't tell anyone."

As soon as Jens landed in Bettendorf, he established the core group of training partners and friends that he wanted to be with. Jeremy Horn and, months later, Spencer Fisher were two of those guys. Many considered Jeremy to have the most amazing mind when it came to technique and strategy. When I asked him to describe his friendship and thoughts about Jens, he said, "Jens has one of the most driven mindsets of anyone. He would train so hard it amazed the rest of us. I was never a star high school athlete. I just have a good brain for the sport of MMA. I am able to see what needs to be done and set a great strategy. Jens was a perfect teammate. He was physically gifted and would quickly learn anything I taught him. One of the best examples of this was the bout against John Lewis. It took us a week to develop the game plan and took Jens eleven seconds to win the match. We just made an incredible team."

Just one day after Jens won his world title, he and Pat traveled to North Carolina to an MMA seminar. It was at this seminar where they were introduced to a guy named Spencer Fisher. Spencer had watched the UFC event the night before and witnessed Jens's victory. After hearing about the seminar, he packed up and made the six-hour car ride to attend.

Spencer told me the reason he wanted to meet these guys was because of what he saw as he watched the event. "They were like a pack, a family, as they walked down the hallway together. I knew they were united. I could sense what a remarkable team they had developed. It sold me on the seminar. After meeting them, I knew I would join their team. Within days, I decided I would move to Iowa."

"After I arrived and practiced with the guys, I noticed that no one could keep up with the smallest guy in the room. No one could hang with Jens. Feeling brave, and knowing I had over thirty pounds on him, I decided to spar with Jens. I've told this story a hundred times. I tell everyone that I wore my nose on my shirt that night."

As he laughed through his next few sentences, Spencer mentioned that it was quite some time before he matched up with Jens again. He wanted his nose to remain on his face.

Spencer used his first couple of years at the Miletich camp trying to learn from Jens. He recounts, "I wanted to emulate him. I wanted to follow his lead. Every time I stepped in the ring, I wanted Jens in my corner." While Spencer and Jens became like brothers, and connected right away, not every relationship at the gym started this way. Some took quite a bit longer to develop.

Jens could also make sure that new guys earned their stripes. To become legitimate in the MFS (Miletich Fighting Systems) elite gang, you must pay the applicable dues, and the currency is not monetary. A few years back, a literal giant walked into the gym and wanted to fulfill a dream. He wanted to be a champion. This goal, however, was not a new one; the existing team had heard it before. He stood six feet eight and tipped the scales north of three hundred pounds. His name was Tim Sylvia.

As Tim and I began to discuss Jens, I found myself coming to grips with his sheer size. The last time I hopped on a scale,

I remember the reading was about one hundred and fifty-five pounds. He had eight inches on me and almost double my body weight. I looked down at his hands and thought, for a fleeting moment, "This guy could kill me with one punch."

After I dismissed the unlikelihood of my visit to the morgue, we visited, talked, and laughed. I found Tim warm and engaging; he was nothing but kindhearted and funny.

He spoke with a heavy Maine accent, the kind where "car" becomes "cah." Sylvia started in: "When I first men Jens, I remember a loud, outspoken guy. I noticed he trained harder than anyone in the gym. He always outworked his opponent. He was in better condition, had a bigger heart and much more determination. We got off to a rocky start. He was hard on me. I couldn't tell whether it was because he was a prick or believed in me. Perhaps it was both. Even when he was tough on me, I wanted his respect. I wanted his approval."

Sylvia knew Jens was a leader and didn't want to make waves. He realized that obtaining an endorsement from him wasn't going to be easy and would require training like an animal, making sure that he never complained. He took a few Pulver tongue lashings and worked his tail off. After winning his first fight in the UFC, he proclaimed, "That was for you Jens."

As their relationship became less cantankerous, Tim had an opportunity to compete in Hawaii. It was called Super-brawl, and, if he was successful, it would be a breakthrough weekend for Sylvia. He wanted to win. He wanted to triumph. He wanted Jens Pulver in his corner.

Jens made the trip with him and told Tim that, if he listened to his advice, he would win. As it turns out, Sylvia had four fights that day and administered four crushing knockouts. He won the entire event. Immediately after disposing of his last opponent, he made his way back to the corner. What he experienced next breaks him up even today. Sylvia explained, "Jens was crying. He grabbed hold of me and told me how proud he was. He said I deserved it more than anyone. Jens said he had been hard on me because he believed in me. He wanted me to be the best I could be."

Tim Sylvia, current heavyweight world champion, finished: "I used to call him Oscar the Grouch. Today, Jens Pulver is one of my best friends. He is the brother I never had. There is nothing in this world I wouldn't do for him."

The man that kept all the puzzles pieces together, not surprisingly, was Pat Miletich. He not only has to manage his training facility and business, he has to manage the guys. And although he doesn't play favorites, there's a special place in his heart for Jens. Pat explains: "No matter how deep your scars are from life, you can use these as motivation. Jens had a tough life as a youngster but did not use it as an excuse for not succeeding. Most people don't succeed because of a fear of failure, while successful people have failed a thousand times before hitting the mark."

Pat goes on: "Here's a kid who sacrificed all the comforts of living and security to jump a train and pursue a dream. That's total commitment. I have always believed that the best way to see what's on the other side is to throw your hat over the fence and go get it. The strongest people in the world are the ones willing to take that chance."

Pat transitions from a few of his favorite Jens qualities to a couple that drive him crazy: "He is a creative guy, with passion and fire. He's also as bullheaded as you can imagine. At times, he can be like one of those mules with a rope around its neck. The harder you pull on the rope, the more its heels dig into the dirt and rock, deliberately going against the grain."

Pat and I began to laugh out loud at the visual. I think we both replaced the picture of the donkey and inserted Jens into our imagination. The humor was in the truth. Jens could be as stubborn as a mule, but it didn't matter to us. We've accepted him as he was, heels dug in or not.

As ornery as Jens can be on occasion, the brilliant light of his goodness shines through. On countless occasions, Pat has witnessed his loyalty, kindness, and decency. Jens once told me that after Pat lost two of his brothers in a relatively short period of time, Jens approached Pat with a promise. He told Pat that, although he could not replace his loss, he would be his brother. Although guarantees are hard to come by, this one was solid. This promise was unbreakable. He indicated that, whatever the future held, through good or bad, for the rest of his days on this earth, Pat had a brother in Jens.

There was a particular story Pat shared that struck me as a powerful metaphor for Jens's life. The tale enveloped so many characteristics of his existence, including bravery, uncertainty, excitement, unpredictability, spirituality, madness, energy, violence, trust, fear, laughter, risk, and survival. It also reminded me that how you view the situation is *always* your choice.

Since Jens grew up in the Northwest, tornados were not part of his upbringing, at least the naturally occurring ones. One day a few years ago, Pat looked at his to-do list for the day and deemed it boring and uneventful. An aggressive weather pattern was forming, and Pat reckoned it required some further investigation. He called Jens and asked him if he wanted to join him for a ride. Pat was going storm chasing. It seemed like a reasonable and prudent way to spend the day.

Jens came to the conclusion that he was tough enough for the trek and accepted the invitation. He and Pat headed west on Interstate 80 and pursued the southwest corner of the storm. As they approached inclement weather, they tuned into a local radio station and carefully listened for updates. To their amazement, the weather expert suggested that all listeners seek shelter and stay off the roads. Pat, grinning from ear to ear, said, "It was the best wall cloud I had ever seen. We attempted to get out in front of the storm but ran into dead-end roads and barricades. By this time, I could see Jens starting to freak out. There was heavy rain, hail, and intense winds ... branches from trees were flying through the air, along with chunks of barn siding and other debris. My heart was pounding."

It is true that Pat and Jens had come a long way from their initial car ride. However, Jens had memories of Pat's cavalier attitude with regard to travel policies. As the roads were peppered with flash flooding and the radio announcer changed his tone to "Get your ass in the basement," Jens was no longer thrilled with his earlier decision to accompany Pat Miletich, tornado-chasing aficionado.

Pat further described the voyage: "By now, I had my wife on the phone, and I described the scene. Perhaps that wasn't the wisest thing to do. She began to cry and fear for my safety. Jens could hear just enough through my cell phone, and he started whining as well. I thought, 'Oh, my God, what I am going to do here? I have my wife breaking down, and Jens is in full panic mode!' I finally told them both to relax and we'd be fine. 'Clearly, [grin] I have everything under control.'"

What Pat said next was the item that figuratively knocked me out of my chair. It summed up life in general. He provided sage advice to Jens, to all of us. The kind of advice that could be on bumper stickers, billboards, and greeting cards. Pat looked over to Jens in the passenger's seat and calmly stated, "Enjoy the storm, Jens; enjoy the storm."

Kingdom Assignment—
Hughes Style

On a beautiful fall Wednesday, I was making my weekly jaunt to Pat's gym. There were clear skies and above average temperatures. As the wind whipped through my vehicle and John Legend's voice thumped through the speakers, I had the feeling that today would be special. In recent weeks, the Wednesday group had been astonishing, and I left each week with optimism, joy, and hopefulness. I hoped that it was God's plan for us to unite and hoped that he had something great up his omnipotent sleeve.

Each Wednesday, my goal was to show up about ten minutes early and assemble the chairs, partly to be helpful and ensure that we started on time, yet the driving force was to place my keys on an acceptable chair selection. Not to beat a dead horse with the chair thing; however, germaphobes have their limits, too. I was certain that one of those black chairs would be the causal link to an outbreak of monkey pox.

As I opened the double doors to enter the wrestling room, odds were that my knees would buckle. The toxic and noxious aroma of thick, soaked-on-the-walls sweat sometimes caused me to gag. If the rest of the team knew the truth about how fragile I was, I faced possible banishment for being a weak sister. Not that I truly believed I would be ostracized; I just didn't want to take the chance. So, although it was against the unwritten rules, I cracked the door at the back of the gym to let some fresh air into the room.

I was not the only one to notice the offensive smell. Many a comrade had shared his feelings on the topic. Surrounded by a bunch of silent weasels, I simply possessed the nuts to address this oppressive, unchangeable attribute of our sacred meeting. As fresh, Grade D breathable air entered, I sensed a small victory.

After Keith opened with a prayer, the discussion transitioned into how Jesus would consistently help the less fortunate. Instead of hanging out with the in crowd, he would find a way to show up with the beggars, tax collectors, and even prostitutes: the unloved. As always, Jesus delivered mercy, grace, and healing to a dying world. It's interesting that, two thousand years later, the same concept is relevant and germane. One of the guys chimed in with a certain phrase that resonated with many of us. He said, "Use every day of your life to spread the Gospel and only use words if necessary." The message was simple. Lip service doesn't add up to much, and actions speak louder than words.

About twenty five men were in attendance today; and two seats to my left, I noticed ol' Square Jaw counting them off, one by one. With a certain quietness and humility, Matt Hughes had an announcement to make. Unprovoked and unrehearsed, he made it known that, next week, he would bring in a stack of hundred dollar bills. Each of us would receive one C-note and were to use the money to advance God's kingdom. Kevin, Keith, and I could barely sit still. Eighteen months earlier, our church had done the exact same thing.

Although Matt was loosely familiar with the concept, there was a book called *The Kingdom Assignment*, which, five or six years earlier, was the genesis for this concept. Denny and Leesa Bellesi, pastors at a southern California church, called one hundred people up to the front of their congregation. Then, they promptly passed out a one hundred dollar bill to each of them. Usually, churches are known for collecting money; so the originality of handing it out caught most people's attention. There were three rules for these unsuspecting recipients:

1) This was God's money.
2) They needed to invest the money to advance God's kingdom.
3) At the end of ninety days, each person would report back with the results of the investment.

Another underlying idea of the assignment was to get people behind the movement and multiply the initial seed money. This idea relates to the parable of the talents, in chapter fifteen of the book of Matthew. Participants were encouraged to contact family, friends, and acquaintances in the hopes they would contribute to the mission. They could donate their time, talent, or treasure; and together, everyone could multiply the one hundred dollars many times over. Keith mentioned that by the time the ninety days had expired at our church, we had raised over $90,000 in advancing God's kingdom. The enthusiasm of what was to develop detonated in the room. An inferno of ideas began to launch. Fighters, business owners, teachers, salesmen, military men, athletes, pastors, and students were dripping with excitement; kingdom assignment—Hughes style—had commenced.

As the days and weeks passed, we utilized a few minutes at the opening of each meeting to obtain updates. It was exciting to learn the diversity and range of assignments. Each one had the thumbprint and uniqueness of the originator. Just twenty months earlier, I sat in a small office with Pat, Kevin, Anthony, George, and Keith. The six of us read from a book and pondered our relevance and purpose. I always felt we had something special. I felt we had a chance to change the world.

At present, there had been over one hundred and twenty men who had attended the group, and a regular week toggled between twenty-five and thirty-five attendees. These men had determined, as I had, that Wednesday at 11:00 AM was the most significant hour of their week. Guys who had never before experienced fellowship like this waited on the edges of their chairs to provide updates on their kingdom assignments.

Matt Pena was one of the first to complete his endeavor. He obtained a pair of UFC gloves that had been autographed by many of the most notable names in the league, placed the gloves on eBay, and, by the end of the bidding, harvested over twelve hundred dollars. He donated the money to a high school football player who was recently paralyzed on the playing field. In addition to their son receiving a life-changing injury, the boy's family was inundated with a heap of medical bills. Matt didn't know the family, and they didn't know him. He simply wanted to pay it forward; he wanted to make a difference.

One guy purchased clothes and essentials for a homeless man in his hometown. Another started a campaign to collect used sporting goods for kids who couldn't afford new. As odds would have it, a local pastor named Patrick attended only two sessions at the Wednesday group all year; one of the days was when Matt Hughes handed out forty one hundred dollar bills. Patrick raised enough money to purchase a van full of groceries for a woman in need. An eighty-six-year-old ex-military man sent a dollar bill to one hundred men overseas, with a note of encouragement. Yet another person took a flock of children to the movie *The Nativity Story*. After the film was over, he gathered the kids and discussed the importance and significance of the story.

Spencer designed and sold a new T-shirt; his funds would be donated to his cause. A man named Phil approached his friends in his quest to raise money for the Quad Cities Prayer Center. A college student placed boxes, at various locations in town, to gather blankets, hats, and scarves for those in need. One man raised money and purchased groceries for several families who possessed bare cupboards. Another individual purchased Christmas presents for a man living under a bridge. A ministry in Lithuania was the choice of charity for another person.

My friend John has embarked on what he calls The Ivan Project. On his last trip to Chicago, John and his wife, Pam, met a homeless man named Ivan. After the couple purchased some hot food for him, Ivan displayed such gratitude that John hasn't been the same since. He contacted his daughter Aubrey, a second-year college student. Now, ten of her friends are behind the venture. If John has anything to do with it, there will be fifty individuals, just like Ivan, who benefit from his assignment.

Keith produced a music CD and sold copies to raise funds for his charity. Yet another man knew of an impoverished single mother who needed clothes, food, and money. He challenged his friends, family, and coworkers to get involved and participate. His kitty soon grew to nearly a thousand dollars.

A buddy of mine named Bob went to a local school and focused on troubled boys. His wife taught at the school and had heard countless stories of broken homes and the scarcity of role models. Bob met with the principle and started a lunch mentoring program. His goal was to recruit guys from the Wednesday group and have one student taken to lunch each week. It would be a forum for the child to express any burdens on his heart. Bob and his recruits wanted to show these kids that someone cared.

A fellow named Paige utilized his hands and his heart. He took his one hundred dollars and purchased ingredients to bake pies. His enterprise has exploded, and the orders keep rolling in. Yielding a modest ten dollars per pie, he continues the cycle of baking, buying more ingredients, and baking some more. The charity he has selected is an orphanage in Romania. For only five dollars, he can purchase and provide a bicycle for one of the children. It wouldn't surprise me if, by the end of Paige's assignment, he provided bikes for one hundred kids. My prediction is that his investment will return a hundred bikes and a million or more smiles.

I felt amazed as I watched these stories unfold and saw the pride that accompanied the missions. The dividends paid to one's spirit are overwhelming. George, who was in charge of tallying the stories, informed us that well over one thousand people had been touched by these endeavors. The recipients were not limited to the United States, as people in Africa and Europe also saw what a motley crew in Bettendorf, Iowa could deliver with God's help. All of these assignments were significant, and each of these men was doing his part to make a difference. Some of the quests were on a smaller scale, and some of the undertakings were grand. A couple of the guys felt their work would go unnoticed, while a few others believed their efforts would change lives. And, although it might have seemed like a long shot, a few of the men even believed in miracles.

Miracles Can Happen

Jens called me on my cell phone: "Yo, are you going to be with me on Saturday night?" Not knowing exactly what he was asking, I actually had planned on going to Keith's house to watch the UFC event. Matt Hughes and Tim Sylvia would each be defending their titles, and another Wednesday attendee, Sherman Pendergarst, was making his UFC debut. The Miletich men were blanketing the card that night, and we were all extremely excited.

"Where do you need me, Jens? What's going on?" Jens was scheming. He explained it was an extension of the kingdom assignment that he, Pat, and Matt had developed. He wanted to know if I would be his right-hand man at a fundraiser on Saturday night. A local company, which committed to donating nineteen thousand dollars to the Miracles Can Happen Boys Ranch, had reneged on their sponsorship. They had been notified that the word God or Jesus was displayed on something affiliated with the organization, and they pulled the funds.

The ranch was a home-style setting where troubled boys from ages fourteen to eighteen could stay. The founder, a man named Jim Fry, taught the boys about hard work and Christian morals. In many cases, if it were not for the boys' ranch, these kids would end up in correctional facilities or even prison. In the language of poker players, Jim was "all in" when it came to the Lord. His entire life was dedicated to the ministry and helping young men change their lives for the better. Desperately counting on this donation, Jim and the ranch now needed support more than ever.

Once Pat, Jens, and Matt decided on the boys' ranch, Pat picked up the telephone and instantly displayed his leadership abilities. His idea was to have his fighters donate a boatload of autographed shirts and sell these to raise money. This would take place on a couple of different days, at a few unique locations. Tantamount to a general calling on his troops for a much-needed mission, the compliance came without hesitation, and support swelled. Within two days of the concept, nearly a thousand shirts were available from Tim "the Maine-iac" Sylvia, Matt Hughes, Pat Miletich and MFS Elite, "Ruthless" Robbie Lawler, Josh "the Dentist" Neer, and, of course, Jens Pulver.

Local establishments would televise the upcoming UFC event, and we decided to dispatch crews at two Quad Cities locations. Instead of hanging around with buddies, watching the bouts, this had morphed into a night of charity. All of the money raised on Saturday would be given to Jim Fry at the ranch. Pat's final call was to a local dealership, Quad City Suzuki, and the owner came through in spades. Beyond expectations, he informed Pat that the business would double the amount of money he raised for his kingdom assignment.

Back to my phone conversation, I could hear the excitement in Jens's voice, crackling through my cell phone: "Tim, can you imagine handing over a check for ten grand? It's all about the kids, brother. It's all about the kids."

I replied, "Jens, you tell me when and where, and I'll be there."

"Alright, man, I appreciate ya. Talk to you tomorrow; I'm out." Click.

Another conversation with Jens had proven to be another example of shock and awe. He shows generosity, selflessness, and giving. Jens gives ceaselessly. The dozens of shirts that he would be donating constituted one of his main sources of income. The revenue from these shirts could add up to rent payments; yet it took less than a second for his decision. And even more impressive, he acts blissfully and without looking back.

On the night of the bouts, I linked up with Jens and two other guys. We joined my friends Bob and my wife's boss of many years, a guy named Jay, both attendees of our Wednesday group. At another location were George and my buddy Gary, the infamous minister of malaprops. Between the two sites, we did fairly well, and the shirts were a hit. A few weeks later, Pat and the MFS Elite boys held a three-hour session at Quad City Suzuki, which turned out to be a gorgeous success. At the fundraiser, the dealership owner, John Palmer, walked over to Pat and calmly handed him a check for ten thousand dollars.

The total for the combined endeavor was north of sixteen thousand dollars.

When Matt Hughes handed out a few hundred dollar bills and our kingdom assignments began, no one could have predicted the outcome. A month later, four hundred dollars became sixteen thousand. Jim Fry was in attendance at the Suzuki fundraiser that day. He told us that others had heard of the nineteen thousand dollar shortfall and became inspired to give. Between Pat's kingdom assignment and other recent donations, the boys' ranch brought in nearly twenty-seven thousand dollars in one month.

The day Jim Fry found out the sponsorship money had been pulled, he was devastated, but he was also determined. And like so many times in his life, he trusted God to deliver. He has always believed that *miracles can happen.*

If you want to change the world, you cannot sit on the sidelines. Inaction is not the solution. Sometimes, if you want to see more clearly, if you want your vision to be vivid, all you have to do is open your eyes.

20/20 Vision

It was a cool, breezy Thursday night. I had finished a good, solid ten miles of running and a quick shower. After dinner, I assembled my kids in the living room. My son, Steele, was making an obstacle course with the couch cushions, and daughter Macey was practicing dance moves she had learned in class earlier that day. Her moves were imaginative and flowing, yet I was struck by the fact that she had been wearing the same outfit for the last three days. The dress was named Pinky-Reddy, which was derived from the only two colors the garment had to offer. This complex naming convention was an extension of such characters as Dolly the doll and Lizzy the lizard. Directly after a "Daddy, you weren't watching the whole time; you need to watch again," my cell phone rang.

Kevin was on the line and asked the obligatory, "Whatcha doin', brother?" I informed him of the evening's rather lively schedule, and he mentioned that he had just received a call from one of the guys from the Wednesday group.

There is almost an unconscious reflex that everyone calls Kevin first. It has never been formally announced that Kevin is the go-to guy; it just happened that way. He has an unmatchable quality of peace about him and is not self-absorbed enough to even notice; but after meeting him for fifteen minutes, you would trust him with your life. The guys immediately notice that he is different—good different.

The phone call tonight was from Tai, a soft-spoken Asian fellow who had moved to Bettendorf from the borough of Queens, New York. He was diminutive compared to some of the other athletes; however, his heart and passion for coaching troubled kids outsized the average man. Tai had a master's degree in education and could relate to kids who had never eaten with a silver spoon.

If you visited Pat's gym and saw Tai with the gloves on, you might make the mistake of judging a book by its cover. A visual drive-by may produce the perception of a small, sweaty kid, donning torn workout gear, his five days of unmanicured whiskers producing a scruffy, unkempt appearance. His face owned a few battle scars from recent clashes on the mat and in the ring. Make no mistake about it, though; this kid was tough. Jens had told me about this guy's heart and determination. While many others before him had come and gone because they couldn't take the heat, Tai was still rolling.

Yet, like so many of the guys in the group, the fighter mentality was tempered by an inner feeling of fear and uncertainty. Tai dialed Kevin's number a couple of times and proceeded to hang up each time. He wanted to talk with someone, confide in someone, yet had absolutely no practice asking others for help. Throughout his whole life, he had concluded that reaching out would be considered a sign of weakness, which he was determined to avoid. However, he wanted this time to be different. His virtual bank account of trust had been flushed with deposits over the last few months. His brothers in the Wednesday group had demonstrated—through actions, not words—that he could count on them for anything. Not that any member was particularly qualified for such counseling or feedback. What mattered more was the willingness to listen. The invitation for any discussion remained open.

Tai's retina had been shattered in a recent bout, and his vision was failing quickly. He was scheduled to have emergency surgery the next morning, and he felt terribly anxious. He simply needed a friend that night, someone to talk with, who might say everything was going to be OK. Perhaps equal to the trepidation of losing his eyesight was the possibility of never again being able to compete in MMA. This was a huge and unplanned event in his life. The dreams of becoming a champion might soon be over.

Tai called Kevin and asked if he had a few minutes for him. Kevin and his daughter Grace were at Pat's gym for her beginner self-defense class, so he told Tai he would call him back. This was only partially true. Kevin phoned me and Keith, then briefed us on the situation. Moments later, Kevin was on his way to pick me up, and Keith hopped in his car to meet us. We arrived at Tai's residence, disembarked from our vehicles, and the three of us approached his door.

With respect to dogs, I have a simple, uncomplicated point of view. I basically like mine but have no compulsion to foster a relationship with someone else's dog. Not to sound callous or unfeeling, it's just that other people's dogs are typically a hassle. I get irritated if I'm at someone's house and a dog decides to mess with me. Whether the animal jumps on me, licks me, leaves drool on my sleeve, is overly aggressive, overly playful, or finds it necessary to hump my leg, it's all the same: I'm annoyed. As fate would have it, as we approached Tai's house in an unlit alleyway, I could sense my dog-irritation buzzer would be sounding.

Although the alley was equivalent to cave darkness, I could sense something askew. I believed I saw one or two pit bulls. The fact that I didn't know the actual count concerned me since it—or they—were moving with lightning speed. I couldn't predict with certainty what would happen next, but I narrowed it down to two possible options: a leg humping or a fatal attack.

To my relief, I heard Emily and Spencer "the King" Fisher emerge from the shadowy abyss and order the allegedly ferocious creatures to stand down. I suddenly remembered that someone had previously told me Tai had other roommates. Aside from living with Spencer, Tai's dwelling also housed the likes of Josh "the Dentist" Neer. I found this all rather curious; with three of the toughest mixed martial artists around, who needed a pit bull? Of all possible addresses to break into, a robber would get choked out before finding the first jewelry box. Nonetheless, Tai appeared at the door, shaking his head, and let us into his room. He sat down on the couch in disbelief. He anticipated that he would receive two minutes of Kevin's Thursday night and thought he was an inconvenience for even calling. Before the three of us walked in the door, he believed no one cared. He was wrong.

I'm always amazed at how similar we all are, once we peel back the onion. Sometimes, all we need is for someone to listen. Most of us want our friends and family to identify with what is truly inside us: our fears, unease, and concerns. We wonder if anyone else copes with these same battles or faces these types of apprehension. In the raw and basic core of our being, we just want to be heard, absent any judgment and without any criticism. We simply want to be heard.

As we sat down in Tai's quaint, modest living space, we didn't have to say anything. I closely watched his eyes and could see his stress and burdens melt away. The scales of dread that had overtaken him were peeling and vanishing, as if he took one collective deep breath and sigh, which lasted for a half an hour. Courage, strength and will replenished his body and soul. Tai spoke for thirty minutes straight. Kevin, Keith, and I just sat and listened. A couple of times, we piped in with open-ended questions, but that's all the collaboration Tai needed. The topics ranged from his fears of losing his eyesight to the uncertainty of his dream of fighting in the UFC. Yet, strikingly more paramount to him, were the kids he had been teaching. More than any of the pending, personal casualties he would be facing, he worried about his upcoming absence from the school. Only after the surgery would the doctors be able to determine the length of his recovery. Therefore, no one knew when Tai would see his students again.

His classroom was comprised of the undesirables. These were the youngsters who had been regurgitated from the standard, traditional schools, many times for justified reasons. These children were from broken, corrupted, and dysfunctional homes. When Tai first started at this school, he thought his name had changed to F--- You, since this is how he was most often addressed. Although it would wear on his patience, he would endure the verbal abuse if it meant getting a chance to have a conversation. Tai knew that he may very well be the last chance any of these kids had before prison or gangs. He told them that he wouldn't abandon them, that he would be there. He told them that they could count on him. He knew that he could make a difference. For these boys, his word was all he had.

Scripture warns of the temptation of seeking praise for doing good works. In Matthew, Chapter 6, Jesus tells us that, if we help others or give to the needy, we ought not to announce our deeds with trumpets. Although it would be generous to do so, if we gave a thousand dollars to the church and promptly declared it to fifty people, that's not what God had in mind. We are to give of ourselves with time, treasure, and talent, without expecting or searching for reward. If we share a story of giving with others, we may have to evaluate our hearts and check our motives. However, I truly believe that, if we distribute our accounts with the goal of inspiring others, this is a worthy reason to do so.

Kevin, Keith, and I did nothing especially profound that night. Our trip to Tai's place was no big deal for us, and we were glad to do it. Our buddy needed someone to talk to, and we provided that forum. What is amazing is that perhaps it *was* a big deal to Tai. The reason I am so eager to describe these events is because of what happened in the upcoming months. Tai had been lonely that night. Loneliness might be the most horrible feeling known to man. I recently read that being lonely is more likely to shorten your life than more obvious things like poor eating habits or lack of exercise. Since I'm a few credits short of my medical degree, I can't speak with authority on the subject, but the passage ended with, "It's better to eat Twinkies with a friend than celery by yourself."

I learned, yet again, that paying it forward changes lives. If we perform random acts of kindness, they are almost contagious to the recipients. Introspectively, they question why someone would demonstrate kindness to them and expect absolutely nothing in return. In many relationships, circumstances, and situations, we expect an underlying quid pro quo. Not here, not this time. After this type of experience, the forces of spirituality and nature take over, and the beneficiaries often want to return the favors, whether dealing with people they know or perfect strangers. Since Tai would never participate in self-congratulatory behavior, he paid it forward and has no idea that many of us know—but we do.

About two months later, Tai was back in New York City; however, this time it wasn't about him. We learned that he had read in the paper that, with a small monetary investment, he could provide dozens of meals to the needy. The fact that he was contemplating helping others was significant. However, the intentionality of who the recipients would be is commanding. Tai's investment would be inherited by the homeless of NYC. And he wouldn't just be dropping the check off; he would be serving the food as well. Tai selected a group of society that had a terrible affliction; they were lonely. Albeit for a fleeting moment, on one autumn night in New York, Tai made a difference. He was able to look at these meager souls, into the shadow of their eyes, and let them know someone cared. Since others had helped him, because others had found the time to listen, this time the tables would turn. On this night, at this soup kitchen, he would provide his eyes, ears, and heart. In the tiniest corner of the world, if he had anything to say about it, no one would be lonely tonight.

Regardless of what happened during his eye surgery many weeks before, one thing was certain: Tai had 20/20 vision.

Jens and Taisei

Flawed

Jesus said, "Come as you are." In the course of our midweek discussions, Keith had pounded this into our heads repeatedly. He had reminded us on a myriad of occasions that, if we choose to come to Christ when we had everything figured out, when everything in our lives was orderly, we would never get there.

For numerous guys, this experience had been the first time in their lives they had been able to open up, discuss their feelings, share their vulnerabilities, and feel safe. We all carried many burdens that we were unwilling to release. Without this band of brothers, many of us would never have been cleansed of the poison that ran through our veins. Often weeping like little kids, the fiercest guys on the globe let down their guard, revealed the crosses they bear, and asked their brothers for heartfelt advice.

Many of us in the Wednesday group have confessed our feelings of unworthiness. We falsely believe that prior actions, mistakes, and sins have created an impenetrable barrier between us and God. We have bought into the lie that, because we have fallen short of perfection, we won't make the cut. We know that many times we feel broken, damaged, and imperfect; we feel flawed. During a conversation with Jens's mom, I was reminded of God's grace and mercy. His forgiveness. His unending patience. His love. His acceptance.

Marlene told me that, many years ago, she had a tremendous amount of guilt and pain in her heart. She felt terrible for what her boys endured. As twisted as it sounded to me, she felt a degree of responsibility for the rage inflicted on her sons. One morning she was on her hands and knees, on the floor of the shower, crying so hard it hurt her chest. She pleaded with God to forgive her for the past. She wanted forgiveness for every time Jens and his brothers got punched, beat on, and horse-whipped. She wanted forgiveness for every time they pissed their pants because they couldn't bear to hear their father's voice. In the midst of her prayer, she remembers hearing a voice in her head: "You are forgiven."

She stopped crying momentarily and replied, uncertainly, "How can you forgive me?"

The voice replied, "Because you asked; you are forgiven *because you asked.*"

Holding Onto the Belt

I run. Almost every day of my life, that's what I do. That's where I process my thoughts, goals, and demons. And I'm not referring to casual jogging; I enjoy more of a sufferfest. After a brief warm-up, it's time to test the heart, time to see if my body can endure what I put it through yesterday, time to run hard, breathe hard, sweat hard, think hard, and examine. And self-examination can hurt worse than twelve hard miles at a redlined pace. Fifty-two weeks a year, regardless of the elements, I run outside. I despise treadmills and wouldn't be upset if legislation were passed to outlaw these machines, which defraud the runner from the true, fully realized experience of running. The panoply of sun, wind, noise, rain, spectators, colors, snow, and landscape are more important to me than the miles I click off. The outside air, even when brutally cold, ripens the experience. Categorically, my soul and spirit reach their highest levels of peace and liberty when I'm running.

At the halfway point of each journey, I usually take a few seconds to recover. If I need to stretch a little, then I stretch. Depending on how I'm feeling, sometimes I indulge in a little water, a shot of GU, or a PowerBar. After a few deep, chest-filling breaths, I take off and head back. The genesis of many of my ideas, concepts, and initiatives are formulated when I'm running. Not surprisingly, I was on a run when I confirmed to myself that I needed to tell a story. I needed to tell the story of Jens Pulver.

I was reflecting on the past year of my life, how quickly it had flown by, and what amazing things had transpired. In terms of friendships, I wondered why God had chosen to bless me with such abundance. Whether it was people I worked with, friends I trained with, guys at church, or guys at the Wednesday group, I was overflowing with the most amazing bonds and relationships. I did not quite understand why God had placed Jens in my life, yet I trusted him and wanted to honor the responsibility.

As I was pounding the pavement and reached the much-coveted runner's high, I came up with the moderately common idea of having some friends over for a brunch. The vivid picture that swirled in my head, time and time again, was to have Kevin, Jens, and their significant others over for a breakfast feast. I wanted the event to be anything but formal. The goal was a casual, comfortable setting among friends. I called Kevin and ran the idea by him. He felt I had a good plan and said he would see Jens later that day. A few hours later, I followed up with Kevin. He had delivered on his promise and successfully lassoed Jens into the commitment.

Michelle and I were eagerly preparing the upcoming brunch, scheduled for 10:00 AM. As I was setting the table, roughly half past nine, my cell phone rang. I saw it was Kevin's number, sort of cringed my face as I looked at Michelle, and wondered if Jens has changed his mind. Kevin quickly informed me there were no issues; he was running a bit behind, but Jens was on the way. Tardiness for T3 was unusual, and I wanted the morning to run smoothly, so I calmly instructed him to get his freaking ass moving. Not wanting to be talked to like a four-year-old, he barked, "Back off; I'll be there soon." About five minutes later, Jens and his friend A. J. had arrived.

Although the trek from his car to my front door takes about thirty seconds, Jens took more than ten minutes to make the trip. With his cell phone attached to his ear, he paced through the front yard, driveway, and porch area, in a nonrepeatable pattern. On many previous occasions, when I had been with Jens, his cell phone was quite active. The callers would range from his manager, Monte Cox, to one of his buddies or a varied range of workout partners. Each time, there would be a certain sort of joking, teasing-type banter that would take place. This call, however, was noticeably different.

I had fired up a fresh pot of Starbucks French Roast and walked outside to take orders. A. J. indicated she would take a rain check; however, she advised me that Jens would surely enjoy a cup. Although it was not even ten o'clock yet, she indicated he was already on his third cup and wasn't ready to stop the fun. I was taken aback when she steered me to the proper amounts of cream and sugar necessary to match his liking. I guess I would have figured he liked it black, extra bold, and none of the sissy additives. Feeling a bit brave, now, I thought about inquiring if he wanted a flaky scone or lightly buttered croissant on the side. As I opened the front door to deliver his coffee, I sensed a seriousness in his voice that warranted some personal space. I took a right turn and hovered around the driveway for a bit, ensuring his privacy. When I glanced over, I noticed a deliberate pacing as he talked. When he was listening, however, he would stop and stare straight at the ground. As he ended the phone call and I walked over to him, he looked up and said just one word: "Mom."

This specific morning was the most beautiful of days, bright sunshine, clear skies and roughly sixty degrees on the thermometer. We were about to enjoy a great meal and give thanks for all of our collective blessings. I didn't know if it was appropriate to ask Jens about the phone call or to see if he was doing alright. I think I said something like, "Are you OK, brother?" It turns out he and his mom were reflecting on the day of the shotgun incident and still, years later, recounted the event with horror and disgust.

Within a few minutes, Kevin, his wife Jennifer, and their two girls, Grace and Madeline, arrived. The atmosphere swung back to joy and gratitude. Jens's father may have corrupted a previous morning, but he wasn't going to spoil this one. We entered the kitchen and noticed Michelle's masterpiece was in overdrive. The banquet consisted of: piping-hot egg casseroles (one vegetarian and one with meat), ham, cheesy hash browns, bananas, grapes, pecan sweet potatoes, three types of home-made bread, orange juice, coffee, hot tea, and a glorious pie, which Paige (from the Wednesday group) had made. Kevin, who was rarely shy around food, was eager to start the feast. As I reminded him not to cut in front of the ladies, a strange but tranquil feeling came over me. I watched in slow motion the natives who had gathered, and I realized that peace and calm had also joined us. Perhaps the most meaningful sustenance in the room was not edible.

There was no rage. There was no sorrow. There was no abuse. There was no screaming. There was no hate. There was simply love. Just the way it was supposed to be, just the way God intended.

The discussion at the table was enjoyable, which is automatic with Jens in the room. We discussed how the next twelve months would be filled with significant events and endless possibilities for all of us. Jens had a few exciting endeavors that could blow things wide open for him. His years of hard work and sacrifice could soon be paying handsome dividends. Kevin was entering the second year of a new profession and understood that his life would be moving at lightning speed. I would be changing careers after fourteen years with the same company. Hence, the next few months would be a combination of the unknown and utter excitement. I believed that God had a new plan for my life, and, if I listened intently, he would reveal what he had in store for me.

I informed everyone at the table that I believed I was called to write this book and there were many reasons to do so. First, and foremost, was to bring glory to God. Reasons two through fifty, although important, are infinitely subordinate to the first. What I have learned, in my brief thirty-six years of existence, is that human beings are generally the same. And no matter how hard we try to convey an aura of invincibility, we all long for the same basic needs. I believe there is a voice inside all of us that speaks to our hearts. It reminds us there is something greater than ourselves. Although we don't totally understand or grasp the concept, we know our Creator does. We all want to be loved. We want to belong. We want to be relevant. We want to be inspired.

As we sipped on our French Roast and consumed the offering, I could see the wheels spinning in Jens's head. He began to review his life's journey with disbelief and amazement. He described how he managed to navigate the intricate minefields of his existence. As he spoke, he also illustrated with his hands, weaving them in and out to demonstrate a circuitous path and dogged road that had led to today. With grit and tenacity, he had survived. There were bumps, bruises, cuts, and literal black eyes; yet, through it all, he was standing.

Jens pondered his recipe for endurance and looked back on a day that changed his very purpose and identity. He was about thirteen years old, and although life was clipping along at lightning speed, Jens and his mom had found a few precious minutes of airtime. She told him a story that inspired him, about a man named Charlie. Here was a figure whom Jens never met, never even saw, yet the wisdom churned in his head for almost two decades, proving, once again, our lives can be changed, restored, and reconditioned by others whose actions or philosophies somehow strike a chord.

His mom met Charlie when she was a little girl, perhaps five or six years old. At the time of their introduction, Charlie was in his mid-seventies. He lived close to her parents' house, and a small, flowing creek commonly bordered their properties. As Marlene made her daily walk along the creek, she began a friendship with Charlie that lasted for nearly twelve years. Their bond survived until his last day.

Charlie had a barn full of horses and introduced Marlene to riding. He had been a rodeo rider, trained trick horses, and, years back, had even been a horse trader. Horses were in his blood. It was a ritual, for Marlene and all of the kids in the surrounding area, to travel to Charlie's each day and ride. Many days, they would be on the top of a horse from sunup to sundown. As she described him to Jens, what she remembered most about Charlie was how much he did for other people. He was always helping, teaching, and telling stories. He was at his best when he was telling a story.

In Marlene's later teen years, Charlie's health began to deteriorate, and, inevitably, he became ill with lung cancer. Charlie was exceptionally grateful for his life. With a wise level of circumspection, and possessing no current regrets, he longed for only one simple thing. He wanted more time. In a world where almost everything can be bought, time was not for sale. He believed there was more for him to accomplish: more lives to touch and more of a legacy to leave. However, as he surveyed the virtual calendar of his life, he understood the precious resource of time was fleeting. As Jens pictured the man's weathered, wrinkled face, he was reminded that the old cliché was true: time waits for no man. He was struck by the fact that, although his own life had been extremely harsh at times, at least he had time, God willing. Presumptively, he had plenty of time.

He brooded over the fact that, of all the resources this world has to offer, our time on this earth is stunningly finite. We never know how much is left or how many more breaths we will take. After hearing the story of a man named Charlie, Jens made a pact with himself. It has been nearly twenty years, and he attempts to honor it each and every day. He didn't want to look in the rearview mirror and have any regrets or admit that he squandered precious days. He didn't want to acknowledge there were times he didn't live his life to the fullest.

At a level too horrible to imagine, without parsing any words, Jens's childhood was brutal. It consisted of getting the sh-t beaten out of him. To understand the abuse means you get sick to your stomach. Your heart aches to hear it. You unsuccessfully attempt to wrap your mind around the fact that it actually happened. When you couple everything together, it's hard to believe he's standing; but he is.

In the last several years, he rose to become a world champion athlete, a feat few will ever reach. Through the Wednesday group at Pat's gym, he has inherited a band of brothers, a troop of men who, with no questions asked, would unconditionally do anything in his best interest. And, although trace amounts remain, he has managed to shed vast amounts of rage, anger, and bitterness. Authoring the mantra that the positive *must* outweigh the negative, Jens now reaches out to help others. He gives back because others have given to him. Jens told me it's simple: "I owe. For every coach, mentor, friend, training partner, for anyone who has ever stepped into my life and helped me, that's why I owe. Because there's a kid out there, somewhere, who's getting his ass torn up every day from a beating, I'm going to be there. I owe. That's all there is to it."

As the sun shined brightly through the dining room window, and morning came to a close, his coffee cup was now empty. He advised us of what he attempts to accomplish each time he opens his eyes in the morning. It's the same goal. He wants every single day to be a story. As he grins from ear to ear, in that animated Jens Pulver way, he guaranteed us: "Some stories you'll be laughing; others you will cry like a baby; but you can be certain of one thing: every day will be a story."

Hills and demons are meant to be conquered.
(Jens and Tim on the Bettendorf bike path)

I will never forget the first day I met him, never forget his ...

tears
struggles
abuse
emotion
suffering
brashness
generosity
authenticity
veracity
moral compass
perseverance
and bravery.

I will never forget *his story.*

Jens Pulver and the Wednesday group will change the world.

If you think this is short term, think we will become distracted or disillusioned, think we will grow weary or that ...

obstacles affect us
naysayers shape us
setbacks influence us
detractors concern us
obstructions disturb us
hurdles upset us
knockouts discourage us
critics dissuade us
fatigue distress us
or the enemy can intimidate us ...

If you think we're going to tap out, I have one word for you ...

Acknowledgments

To my wife, Michelle: you are my everything. Your unconditional love continues to be more than I deserve.

To Jens Pulver for your inspiration and spirit.

The author wishes to thank Lyle W. Hart with Mien Design. You have been my most significant partner in the completion of this book. Your assistance in cover design, content structure, and promotion—as well as your friendship—has been invaluable.

Also, thanks to Keith Nester for your spiritual leadership in the Wednesday group. We would be lost without you.

My sincere appreciation to Pat Miletich, for allowing us to utilize your gym for the purpose of meeting with God. You remain brave and original.

Also, Ogy Blazevic (OgyB), for your amazing photography and talent.

And to Kevin Jandt, for showing me what a Savior truly is.

neverthebook.com   jenspulver.com

978-0-595-43484-8
0-595-43484-3